Paul!

CW01467552

You are the Best
and By the Best

Noel
19/6/19

Global Jihad, Islamic Radicalisation
and
Counter Strategy

Noor Dahri

Vij Books India Pvt Ltd
New Delhi (India)

Published by

Vij Books India Pvt Ltd
(Publishers, Distributors & Importers)
2/19, Ansari Road
Delhi – 110 002
Phones: 91-11-43596460, 91-11-47340674
Fax: 91-11-47340674
e-mail: vijbooks@rediffmail.com
web : www.vijbooks.com

ISBN: 978-93-88161-51-0 (Hardback)

ISBN: 978-93-88161-52-7 (ebook)

Price : ₹ 850/-

Printed at Aegean Offset Printers, Greater Noida, U.P.

Dedication

I dedicate this book to the victims of terrorism who were mercilessly killed at the hands of terrorists who wanted to destroy the world. These victims are the real heroes who gave their lives to protect the world, whether they are in the West, in the Middle East, in Africa or in Asia. Their sacrifices are precious in the world and hereafter. Insha Allah. I would like to thank my family members; Farah Qureshi, Barirah Qureshi and Bayyinah Qureshi, for their cooperation, patience, backing and motivation, I could not have done it without them. I am truly thankful to them.

–Noor Dahri

Contents

Introduction

The Latin word "Radis" or "roots" means buried at the root of fundamental. It shows that a radical is a person who wishes to bring the fundamental, political and social change and therefore radicalisation is a mindset by which people adopt extreme views and beliefs, being prepared to take violent measures for political and religious gains.

Wilner and Duboulos define radicalisation as: "Radicalisation is a personal process in which individuals adopt extreme political, social and religious ideas and aspirations and where the attainment of particular goals justifies the use of indiscriminate violence, it is both a mental and emotional process that prepares and motivates an individual to pursue violent behaviour. It is interesting to note that radicalisation does not always lead to violence in the initial stages. So, a slow process of radicalisation may take place while there is no realisation of the gravity of the situation.

In contemporary discourse of religious radicalisation, religion is often believed to be at the centre of one's radicalisation. Radical ideas are instilled in common people, who have very little understanding of their own religion, in a way that they consider them absolute. Religious radicalisation can be defined as "a process by which a person or group comes to adopt increasingly extreme religious ideas and aspirations that reject or undermine the status quo, or rejects and or undermines the contemporary ideas and expressions of freedom of choice". Robert Mandel refers to religious radicalisation as, "an increase in and or reinforcing extremism in thinking, sentiments, and or behaviour of individuals and or groups of individuals.

1

Alex Schmid, quoting Dalgaard Nielsen's study, came up with six stages of the process of religious radicalisation: [1] Identifying a problem as not just a misfortune but an injustice; [2] constructing a moral justification for violence (religious, ideological, political); [3] blaming the victims (it is their own fault); [4] dehumanising the victims through language and symbols; [5] displacing responsibility (God or other authorities ordered the individual to commit the act of violence) or diffusing responsibility (the group, not the individual is responsible); and [6] misconstruing or minimising the harmful effects (by using euphemisms or contrasting to other acts which are worse).

Now, the question is, what is the name of the religion of terrorists?

The Political methodology is their religion, whether it is called Political Islam, Right wing, left wing, religious extremism or ethno-nationalism. All these groups create political violence in order to achieve their political ends.

The political methodology is actually a religion, the religion of the terrorists aims, the religion that provides them a valid justification to take others' lives. Terrorists use the religion as a political ideology to be dominated in the world whether it has a religious background, nationalist background, white supremacy or political power game. What is the religion actually? It is a combination of beliefs or faiths that individuals possess inside his/her minds. For example someone believes in communism and he/she can even give up his/her life to achieve certain benefits from that ideology, so, if this is the case; he/she worships such ideology or the creator of the ideology. The communism became a religion for communists who blindly follow the ideology of communism.

After three years of hard efforts, education and experience, I am able to present this most valuable knowledge to my readers about global terrorism and violent extremism. The slogan "Terrorism has no religion", which we are listening and reading everywhere, but one thing I am convinced is that "Indeed Terrorism Has a Religion".

Whenever, I present my idea that "Terrorism has a religion", I get strong criticism, especially from my Muslim community. Their argument is that "Islam is a religion of peace; therefore, terrorism has no room in Islam". I do not have any doubt that Islam has no room for terrorism or violence, however, Muslims do use the name of Islam in relations to create violence and mischief. Therefore; I have no other option except to declare that "Terrorism Has a Religion".

In the last few years, I was assessing the entire world, what is happening in the world, who is doing what and what are the reasons behind these bloodied wars and violence that lost millions of lives. I came to the conclusion that Humans have always used violence to get power, either in religion, in politics, in countries or among the nations. Humans want to rule over people by hook or crook. So, they changed the peaceful ideology into violent ideology and started spring fire in the name of whatever is their political or religious ideology.

In my forty plus life, I had many changes in my faiths such as a religious extremist, a secular believer, Marxist/socialist activist and now a moderate religious promoter. I have enough personal life experience to assess the religious and political extremism. I have travelled from Pakistan to Afghanistan and to Kashmir, a journey from pro-Jihadist to anti-Jihadist.

Some people have theoretical knowledge of what terrorism is and how to counter it and some people have practical experience of what extremism is and how to counter radicalisation. I have both knowledge of it as I spent some time in Afghanistan and Kashmir with Jihadists and participated in some violent clashes and have also studied counter-terrorism at ICT- Israel. So, in this scenario, I can sense from miles what terrorism and extremism are and why or/how an individual becomes radicalised.

People need to understand that hateful and violent ideology is generating a variety of messages in their mind process. This is a pure violent psyche that needs to be cured by positive and cognitive mind process with nonviolent messages. Therefore, I

3

have put more light on the ideological process so that when it changes, it can be returned to its original peaceful shape.

In my book, I have included four major chapters:

1. Global Jihad

2. Suicide Terrorism

3. Radicalisation

4. Media Terrorism

There are many subchapters as part of these major chapters. I have also put light on Right-wing terrorism, left-wing terrorism and ethno-nationalism along with religious terrorism. I have drawn a whole picture in my book, where readers can easily see the clear transformation from a religious movement to political movement. Readers will also notice that I have discussed Islamic terrorism very much because nowadays, it is the main issue from the Taliban to Al-Qaeda to ISIS.

I hope readers will enjoy reading my book which is no doubt my life experience and knowledge in extremism and the counter-terrorism fields. As an ex-policeman in the London police department, I can better judge the psyche of criminal whether he/she is ordinary criminal or a high-ranking criminal such as terrorist because terrorism is itself a crime. I pass my special thanks to Musa Khan Jalazai, a prominent author and Tahir Mehmood of Norway, a specialist of Radicalisation for their great advice and help that they provided me in authoring this.

Thank you for reading the book.

Noor Dahri

Founder & Exec. Director

Islamic Theology of Counter-Terrorism (ITCT)

January 2019

Chapter 1

Radical and Extreme Ideology

Ideological Factors

There are a large number of books and journals that discuss provocation and the effectiveness of terrorist's strategies, but still we know little about their tactics and ways of attacks. The basic idea is that provocation is of much importance in terrorist operations. Terrorists are trying to avoid provoking state but favour to provoke citizens against the state. The basic factor in the effectiveness of terrorist strategies is provocation, which requires a forceful response from the state. Forceful response to a terrorist attack carries costs to the state in addition to those incurred from collateral damage. For instance, states with more resources and greater capacity will find forceful response less costly to employ. According to the journal of international security (2012):

> "There are five principal strategic logics of costly signalling at work in terrorist campaigns: (1) Attrition (2) Intimidation (3) Provocation (4) Spoiling (5) Outbidding".

Terrorism is closely related to power. In most cases, we can observe this by how terrorist groups have power over certain areas or groups of people by targeting them. For instance, Boko Haram and its attacks in Nigeria. They have spread fear around the country which has given them this feeling of having power. The money circulation in financing terrorism is very important;

however, it depends on the type of terrorism? For instance, narco-terrorism clearly has a desire of achieving high economic benefits. But I think in other cases the need for money is just because these groups need to finance themselves.

Many terrorist groups have/are using religion in order to establish power and control over people. They "take advantage" of people's situations and beliefs to convince them that Radicalisation is necessary to achieve goals (and a better life for them perhaps?). What is an understanding of "illiterateness in terrorism"?

If we mean people who join terrorist organisations are uneducated or illiterate, then I will say that many supporters who join terrorist groups such as ISIL have diplomas and higher education. Of course, there is a percentage of people who are uneducated and they perhaps may be easier to persuade because they have a closed mentality. In many cases, they live under poor conditions and feel that they have no opportunities in society and have nothing to lose. These elements call grievances.

I guess that are the ones who are truly committed to the cause and do what they do for the goal of their ideology. But we have to pay attention to the fact that in most of the cases the ideological goals are about power. For example; ISIS objective is to impose a global caliphate and for this, they will need to take the power and seize all the money they could to survive longer. I didn't see much power without money around the world. I'm not trying to legitimise terrorist pursuit of money and power, but trying to show that in most of the cases they are a kind of criminal with an ideology. Radical leaders are just trying to get money and power by using the 'quest of significance' of people who are easily manipulated and are constantly searching their significance and importance in their lives, but these leaders aren't preoccupied about the world's environmental, political, economic or religious concerns, although they try to convince everybody else about their consternation, but in the end, they're just looking forward to becoming powerful or rich or even both. Sometimes it's just their egos and they try to convince themselves about their importance in this world and the way they might become heroes by saving us. Prof Neumann (2010) attempted to address a specific distinction in this research on "Radicalisation and De-radicalisation" with the focus on terrorists in the prison system in 15 countries, including, Afghanistan, Israel, the United Kingdom, Pakistan, Saudi-Arabia, Yemen, and the United States among others. Prof Neumann (2010) says: "The principal difference between politically motivated offenders and 'ordinary' criminals lie in their intention. While 'ordinary' criminals commit crimes in pursuit of selfish and/or personal goals, politically motivated offenders believe that they are acting on behalf of a certain group, society or humanity as a whole." Interestingly, Prof Neumann described the behaviour of whether political or ordinary individuals, in this context of terrorism as criminal behaviour but was careful to assert "Not all politically motivated offenders are terrorists, but all terrorists are politically motivated offenders."

This distinction burdens us to mindful in using a "conveyor belt" analysis concerning power and money relationship with terrorism.

Many groups, since the beginning of human history, have fought for power and wealth without this self-annihilation strategy of terrorism, especially suicide bombings, to escape the reality of accountability. No doubt that this should inform us that terrorism is more than just power and money. How will a terror gain power or wealth when such an individual is willing to commit suicide for a cause? As Prof Neumann correctly put it, "Politically motivated offenders commonly distinguish between 'legality' and 'legitimacy', arguing that breaking the law is justified when a particular policy or the entire political or legal system is illegitimate." But these kinds of politically motivated offenders do not engage in brute inhumanity or beheading of defenceless persons, stripping themselves with bombs and blowing up building to murder defenceless civilians, and committing suicide bombings in the name of martyrdom.

Terrorism is political warfare for self-rule and dominance over others, as we see with these Jihadist laws. It's easy (and emotionally taxing) to focus on terrorist successes. We hear and cite the bad news. I think it's also important to discuss the successes in countering terrorism as well. The only way we can have any non-violence is to purpose to the highest of their counsel in their religion that has the authority of the rules and laws in the religion they believe and they will need to change a lot of rules and laws being no more killing and more freedoms within the people. When it is set that nobody is allowed to kill for any reason in their higher order and in the United States where the death penalty is allowed, is changed to no more acceptable reason to kill and all country's sign and agree in a peace treaty for the appreciation of being able to be on this planet and live on this respectably to one another without having to kill. Then there will be almost incidents nobody will ever hear about people dying from other people killing them, only automobiles and travels and accidents.

Ethno -Nationalist Ideology

There is another ideology which is a fast-growing ideology in the west which is ethno-nationalist ideology. I would consider ethno-nationalist ideology a type of separatist ideology.

I am still trying to figure out some sort of possible difference the only thing I came up with is that perhaps separatists focus more on territorial goals and once they have established their territory/borders they move on to develop their own ethnic and linguistic identity.

Whereas ethno-nationalists do it the other way around, they first became a minority in their country/state due to ethnic and/or linguistic reasons; so, in their case first came their identity and then they proceeded to desire of having their own territory. Or perhaps the difference relies on the fact that separatists do not want to live under the government they are in because they feel politically and economically, they are too different or even superior; for instance, they could be the wealthiest state out of all states in the country.

Whereas for ethno-nationals its more about their cultural identity than about governance; what I mean by this is that once they become independent, they share common aspects in their system as when they were still part of a country but the only actual difference is the official language and things like that. I believe it is safe to say that there is considerable overlap, as most separatist movements are ethno-nationalist in orientation (Kurdish groups, the Basque separatists, etc). Occasionally, however, we come across a separatist movement that does not define itself strictly on an ethno-linguistic identity, but on a slightly more inclusive conception of identity. I say it specifically of the case of black separatists and (frequently white) anti-government separatists in the United States, who use a general conception of race (which might include members of many different ethno-linguistic/ nationalist groups) and an intense dislike of their government to demarcate the lines between 'us' and 'them.' There is no language barrier in these somewhat unique instances, and because the idea of the United States is not based historically on an ethno-national idea (the Francs in France, Germanic tribes in Germany, the Visigoths in Spain and Italy, the Celts in Ireland, etc), there are no ethnic boundaries inherent in the U.S.

So, I believe that ethno-nationalist movements are separatist movements (in that they seek some degree of autonomy and self-rule), and the vast majority of separatists are ethno-nationalists, but there can be separatist movements that seek to carve out their own governance based on other ideological reasons and their ideological reasons are too dangerous for the nation as Islamic extremist.

What constitutes an act of Terrorism?

A terrorist beheads someone to instil fear, show that they are powerful and to coerce governments and the general population. Coerce governments to pay them or do as they say or else. To try and turn that Nation's citizens against them and show how weak that Nation is.

That also coerces the general population to join them because they believe that they are strong or do anything, say anything against them this will react instantly in retaliation. A drug cartel beheads someone for many the same reasons as a terrorist, but their lust for money and power.

Though, drug cartels are very some kin to terrorists. Terrorists will engage in criminal activity to raise funds, to pay for training, training camps, weapons, recruitment to achieve the political end etc.... May be that is an over simplification. Clausewitz a Prussian general and military theorist said that "War is the continuation of politics by other means ..."

In that sense, I believe we see terrorism as a real war, where it joins an action and therefore a reaction, where the possibility of breaks dialogues by military action or combat, where each party wants to hurt the other to destroy it because it causes harm, whether physical, territorial, economic, financial, religious or simply not allow that party remains in power political. I say that the legal war is a Radicalisation because violence is used to obtain a goal, which is to defeat the enemy, be it regular or irregular, since the mere fact of moving troops or use intelligence for combat already does legal because the State is involved in an action to counter a threat. ISIS had clearly won the media war. No matter how heinous their crimes were, they are still able to recruit fighters from many nations especially Tunisia, Europe and eastern Asian regions. There does not appear to be any strategy to fight a western propaganda war. One would have thought that the counterterrorism experiences with Al Qaeda would have taught us how to fight the media war. However, that does not appear to be the case, it may be impossible to win this [media] fight. After all, as Christianity shows it's difficult to fight an idea when it claims to right all wrongs and offers a plausible explanation for a particular world view.

Individuals are radicalised by an array of experience. Clark McCauley in his paper "Pathways towards Radicalisation" identifies, twelve mechanisms of Radicalisation and states "not any one of the 12 mechanisms can account for the large proportion of those which have been Radicalised". These twelve mechanisms are as follows:

- Personal Victimization

- Political grievance

- Joining a radical group-the slippery slope (the consequence of being part of the group)

- Joining a radical group- the power of love (love for the cause the comradely)

- Extremity shifts in like-minded groups

- Extreme cohesion under isolation and threat

- Competition for the same base of support

- Within-group competition (splitting of a group where one becomes more radical than the other).

- Competition with state powers- condensation

- Conflict with an out group – Jujitsu Politics

- Conflict with an out group – hate

- Martyrdom

Radicalisation is also a part of the social status of the individual, if he is poor and suffers a continuous humiliation from a group, that individual wants a kind of self-recognition to justify his or her existence. If both fail, which could push the individual to look for a group that could protect him and motivates him, if this is through violence that person will go to that aim in order to survive. In a few years or so in the United States it has been observed intolerance against other people's views especially politically.

We would find those with conservative view extremely skewed to the right and advocating radical things like bombing other countries out of the earth or putting to death those who do not conform to their ideas. During post 9-11 they called traitors and treasonable thoughts of people who did not support the then administration 100%. On the other hand, Liberalism came with a price too especially for those environmentalists' groups. There became incidences of sabotage against perceived things that promoted a lot of wastage in the environment. For example, the destruction of property like big SUVs. And this can also be seen in different countries around the world. Sycophancy has replaced political tolerance and dialogue.

Radicalisation tends to turn violent when an individual's or group's sacred values have been violated or threatened. Individuals will receive a considerable boost to their sense of significance by confronting the group's enemies with little consideration as to the personal risks they may be taking. In this way, the personal or group ideology justifies violence in defence of sacred values and justifies terrorism as an effective and morally acceptable means of significance restoration. Not all individuals who buy into a violence-justifying ideology personally engage in violence; yet, all individuals who commit violence are likely to endorse a violence-justifying ideology. The question is this, are some of the new converts to Takfiri Islam searching for cultural alternatives, counter-therapy, spiritual answers they did not find in their inherited religion?

It has been reported that 90 percent of French youth who go to fight in Syria and Iraq do not have anyone in their family history who followed Muslim tradition; not a grandmother! I am by no means making the case that political Islamic belief is radicalizing, extreme, and an agent of terrorism--just the opposite. Like many Eastern religions, it is a religion of peace, above all. It may be that its better-known reputation in Western Europe, as a mainstream religion, as one that is practiced by productive, non-authoritarian, peaceful communities gives the Takfiris-exploiting ISIS recruiters a legitimacy they would not have were it not for the numerous examples. Millions of Muslims provide to spiritual explorers in Europe. And I am not saying Wahhabism leads straight to terror. The majority of Wahhabis do not aspire to create global terror. "Religious exploitation" or "Grooming the spiritual seeker" is more the process of intentional Radicalisation that ISIS recruiters employ to make an appeal to a wider audience among youth. In regards to the individual Radicalisation, there was an incident that occurred in Aurora, Co, in July 2013 where in a Lone wolf actor assaulted and killed multiple civilians at a movie theatre.

The Individual actor is claiming not guilty by reason of insanity, however, he left detailed plans of his intent to cause mass casualties, wore body armour in an attempt to prevent his immediate death, and he also left booby traps at his residence in order to kill responders in an additional event. That to me screams of premeditation.

Hateful Radicalisation

The question is, does the hate comes before or after the Radicalisation? Do all those Radicalised even know what it is they are getting Radicalised to? I think answers would also depend on how far or distant one is and has been from the conflicts which seem to give rise to the terrorist groups. I do wish we could find some individual psychological profiles to isolate that determines susceptibility to Radicalisation and then, more importantly, the move on to mobilization. Hatred is certainly a motivator for all kinds of acts and terrorism would appear to be high on the list. Again, at what point does a Radicalised person feel enough hatred to torture another person, for instance? America endorsed torture as a method for getting information post-9/11 was that hatred operating? Was that revenge? Was that simply a goal-oriented response? Did we cede our civilized instincts to our need for self-preservation?

I think we must understand what allows a non-terrorist nation to act in ways similar to terrorist groups before we can understand those groups whom we, as a non-terrorist entity, consider to be terrorist. And this is not to imply moral relevancy, but to say, if we can determine how the "civilized" group is driven to act in uncivilized ways, we might get closer to understanding how the "barbaric group" (terrorists) are so driven. "Islamic terrorism" is not understandable, if we understood it; it would be stopped. Indeed, it has been around for several decades if not centuries. And today there is a vacuum created by the terrible implementation of strategies by the West and East. I only know that terrorism is based on fear and the votive insistent from weak-will individuals and vile groups.

Right Wing Extremism

For example, The Ku Klux Klan (KKK) was vile but it's almost none -existent today. The right-wing extremists indeed are around in places such as the jails/prisons so as to offset other sub-sects within the enclosed walls. Individuals need to associate here occurs because of the need to associate and survive in a strange social environment plus the threat of others to do harm. A dog-eat-dog landscape. And perhaps there (right-wing groups) are prominent in certain rural areas of North America or rural areas of the UK.

14

However, the mind-frames of main-stream communities are far away from these individuals. Moreover, in regards to Europe, the European landscape has always had right-wingers. The Second World War did not eliminate them (i.e. Nazis/Fascists).

Less than 1 % were tried and convicted as war criminals. But the politics of Europe have used this right-end element over the years. Over seventeen years living and watching Europe, I have observed this social see-saw. The rise and fall have almost cyclical with good times versus bad. Although, I do not understand the Russians which is extreme but different? In particular, the fairly recent case of Anders Behring Breivik is a poor used in weak arguments to offset a premise or two in a debate. His actions were terrible. He had a manifest, but there were no followers. There was no organized push. It only existed in his head. And I believe it is the result of massive refugees'/immigrants' influxes in fairly stable demographic bases that influenced him. To Breivik, he reacted to a perceived Muslim threat? But the other questions remain: "Who else?" No evidence here. Breivik's incident is almost a Black Swan. A unique expression of violence. But it's not representative of the society he lived. Also, it is not really associated with what is deemed to be right-wing occurrences in Europe (including Greece).

ISIS Ideology against the EU Human Rights Laws

I find religious intolerance and quietness of Muslims more disturbing. The terror and terrorism from Islamist fundamentalists seem constant. [Although, I accept the factoring of over-play by the media in a connected world.] And descent, common individuals know the main characters of this faith than the obscured actor from the right. There is an oxymoron that is going on in the world right now in regards to Islamic terrorism and the West. The West prides itself on internationalism, freedoms, inclusiveness, and our ability to who want to be without heavy interference from government (or ideology). Would a Western Christian from the U.S. last a day in the Islamic State? Never. ISIS stomps out anything different from their beliefs or their rules (Sharia Law).

The very ideology the West was built on, the freedom for everybody to be accepted as who they are in an open society, is exactly what ISIS ideology is directly opposed to. For Muslims, it was of life and beliefs. For the west, it is the same. Both sides have extremes. For an individual to end up on the extremes, the ideology helps fill a void of insecurity or it validates everything.

We have to be susceptible to the message or the narrative changes on us so subtly that we don't even know that we have gone down a certain path for us to change. Ideology is the driver for radicalism because it is an idea and set beliefs, the person just provides the vessel or host for it to continue.

Mind Processing

Islamic Extremism is totally based on the Ideology, without an ideology, no one can take any extreme action in a world. My field of interest is how an ideology could be generated? I personally keep the focus on the mind process that generates an ideology, but how a mind-process works! There are many stages to run the process in the mind. There are some good and some bad stages of the mind process that directly effects a person's behaviour and personality. The question is this, how these stages work? The stages work through the messages which call "unwanted messages". These unwanted messages grow the negative stages that run the negative process of the Mind, and the mind generates the extreme ideology and an ideology generates the extremism and the violent form of the extremism creates violence-based extremists. It does not matter the extremist is a religious, right wing, left wing or ethno-national but the matter is the message that person receives in his/her mind. We have to work hard to stop sending these messages in a person's mind. For example KKK as an organisation does not exist but the ideology of KKK still exists in a different shape because Ideology cannot be changed, it is the same mind process which is the conclusion of unwanted messages.

Behring Breivik is an example of what I am trying to mention here, He was lone, individual, right wing, poor and without affiliated with any group, but he committed the same act as all terrorists did and are doing. He got negative messages in his mind process and these messages generated extreme ideology and he then acted as a lone terrorist. He has not regretted as all Islamic terrorists never regret what they have done because both have a same kind of ideology, but their goals and objectives are different. No matter is who will stop sending these messages in a mind and how?

As long as I know Religion is one of the main causes, but not a whole because a non-religious person could become Radicalised. Some people say, its Governmental policies, some say Poverty, some say unemployment and some say atrocity committed by the regimes so and so. I think every era has a different cause to make people Radicalised for example land strategy, circumstances, political phenomena and non-educational or very low literacy level could be the primary causes behind Radicalisation.

Those people who live in the western world have different causes behind the Radicalisation than those who live south Asian or Middle Eastern countries. I have seen very educated, learned, well established and pure westernised people becoming Radicalised. In my understanding, religion is not the only cause of Radicalisation, because every religion has good principles. Radicalisation or extremism is the misinterpretation of religion, while religion does not support the idea. A man becomes Radicalised when he feels humiliated in society or if he is tortured, like in South Asian culture, his/her relatives are killed or humiliated by the state authorities or a rival group, sect and party.

The Peshawar school attack in Pakistan was revenge of those tribal people whose relatives, sons, daughters or parents were killed by Pakistani security forces in the military operation in

Waziristan region. If we look at the hypothetical conditions of humans in the state of nature- either from the perspective of John Locke or Thomas Hobbes, it would be easy to dismiss religion for the causes of terrorism. Religion, to me, is simply a comforting socialize radical drug for extremists and sadists to commit hideous crimes. Terrorism cannot be explaining through the prism of religion; such exploration misunderstands and poisons appropriate responses to terrorism. In his "Second Treatise on Civil Government" Locke (1690), explained that in the state of nature all men were free "to order their actions, and dispose of their possessions and persons, as they think fit, within the bounds of the law of nature." At this beginning point, there was no organized government but the state of nature was governed by REASON, which assumed that "no one ought to harm another in his life, liberty, and or property."

Is Religion a Factor of Terrorism?

The organised government came into existence as a result of what some scholars would consider as "relative deprivation" when the strong among men began to suppress the weak and dishonoured the law of reason. Therefore, society decided to will their authority into a sovereignty, a ruler- either a King or in modern times a President. It would seem that despite granting authority to a central government, to manage societal resources by providing for the welfare for all people and protecting private interests, we are still trap into the original position that existed in the state of nature, where the strong continue to suppress the poor in most societies across the world, especially in developing and third world nations. This struggle in many societies for upward social mobility has been exploited by crude and inhumane elements in those societies, using religion and other excuses to wage destruction on innocent people.

To undermine terrorism or radicalism, the world must respond to the paralyzing question of social inequality that exists in many societies across the world, ranging from democratic self-government or self-rule and social justice. In an effort to reinforce some of the positive and well thought out comments, I would submit that religion is not the only or the main cause of the Radicalisation. Based in part that the facts state that it has 3 steps. Imagine a frustrated individual that experiences a deep resentment over a real or imagined injustice. Perhaps discrimination or a political cause. The individual may find an ideology that offers him/her support and understands the frustration.

Thus, to share a sense of commonality in achieving a common goal. A feeling of belonging to a team with a common goal or objective. The group as a whole is much stronger than one individual. The group could apply the brainwashing technique to make him/her think that their ideology is the right one. Promoting hatred towards the "enemies" of Islam.

I find it particularly interesting that the Kouachi brothers could kill a Fellow-Muslim as ruthlessly and sadistically as they did (up close as he was already on the ground, shot), but have this tremendous loyalty and passion to defend their adopted religion against an abstraction, a drawing, an idea. Yes, they equated ideas with persons and seemed to have much more feeling for ideas than for human beings. I feel this was a part of their damaged, socio-phatic personalities. They could feel an attachment for ideas, be warriors on behalf of a certain interpretation of a religious "rule," which is not even a rule for all Muslims, and yet cold-bloodedly shoot down defenceless people.

Radicalisation is defined as the process through which an individual change from passiveness or activism to become more revolutionary, militant or extremism especially where there is intent towards, or support for violence. It is including Al Qaeda inspired and related Radicalisation, far right, far left violent movement, and animal rights and environmental extremism. Radical people can be from different level society, high-class society or underclass one. When we take a look at some foreign fighters who were fighting in Syria with Isis, we will conclude that most of them are from North Africa or the Middle East. They were a religious people who old regime torture and put them in jail with no charges or cases, they lack religious freedom, after the Arab spring most of them released from prisons and return to their normal life, but still new governments, instead of adopting them and integrating them into the society to be as a part of that society, still consider them as bad elements and threat to the society.

The result that these people felt that their society treat them with unfair and injustice, with no hope and the felt of that their lives were destroyed, they transfer from normal people to radical ones who hate their society due to the way they got treated.

They felt they found their goal in joining terrorist and radical groups like Isis and other terrorist groups due that they dream to find the justice and the good life in the groups they joined. From normal people to radical ones, to killers who beheaded other innocent ones and kidnapping others and take them as hostage. The main cause for Radicalisation is not only poverty or other things else, but one of the main causes of Radicalisation is the feeling of the rejection of mainstream society and the feeling of injustice.

Terrorism is the fruit of injustice too. The grievance is an important determinant. In a world of growing inequality, where young people can see no future, they are going to be drawn to an ideology which seems to address their grievances (cognitive opening) and hence they will follow (mobilisation).

I find it interesting with ISIS, it seems to play on the hormones of young men by offering them a sabaya (a sex slave) or/ and a wife or wives. A good example is Fabio Pocas 22, a Portuguese convert, who did not reach his dream of becoming a top football player. His boast about the wonder of ISIS is that he has three wives. The latest is a teenager from Holland. A social worker in England, who counsels young women, who wish to go to Islamic State has found that they have an almost nil knowledge of Islam and have the romantic notion that the jihadists are Sheikhs of Arabia. If we do not include all people in a just share of the wealth of society, more terrorist groups will arise. It is all the romantic game, they need virgin brides and women need hero type Jihadi who can protect them.

The environment is important, but perhaps not in this way. There are lots of places in the US under which Broken Windows could be applied but (to my knowledge) are not producing terrorists or violent extremism. Most terrorists come from stable middle-class households (overseas at least). I would argue the environment of the mind is more important. How does the individual perceive his environment? Is it accommodating? Is it restrictive? I think there are many different paths to Radicalisation. Poverty and lack of education do add to the process; however, I see the mechanisms of personal victimization or a close family member by what is thought of as an unjust or unholy government. The idea that a person may be seeking personal revenge or the slippery slope, hanging out and listening and reading radical propaganda. After a while, it may make sense to the person.

However, the most important idea, is this search for personal significance, the idea that I as a person matter, and what I accomplish matters.

The Ideology of Martyrdom

The Radicalised person has had a sense of not mattering, a perceived waste of their life, then suddenly they are given a meaning, not just a significance, but a higher level.... a freedom fighter ... fighter for God....a martyr for the cause.... a great reward in heaven. This desire to matter, to impact those around one, to have personal significance I can see as a driving force, but I think if the individual seeks significance through adopting an extreme ideology that endorses violence and preaches war, we might consider the individual does not just want to matter, the person wants power over other people.

The person wants to matter in a certain way. The young people who become Radicalised by a doctrine that commits them to violent action (whether or not they yet choose to act) might be attracted to violence. They might want significance through yes, cutting off people's hands and beheading people. They want a blood-steeped ideology. What makes the idea of joining an "enemy combatant" force attractive? I am talking about young men, so girls, sure. But I think they are attracted to the idea of carrying heavy arms, wearing scary masks, terrorizing others. They don't seek significance through becoming a published writer, an artist, a rapper--well, actually the Kouachi Brothers had that dream before they traded it in for the dream of becoming terrorists. They wanted to matter, have personal significance, but let's look at the vehicle they were attracted to. It was more than a fancy one or a fast one; it was a killing machine. I think they were attracted to the use of violence, the use of terror, initially to an ideology that embraced violence and terror. I am not talking about religion at the moment. They were attracted to a twisted kind of religion that glorified violence. They could have been two nice Muslim boys attending a traditional mosque. That did not appeal. I think we must go back to history, to remember or to read, as this proves of Radicalisation may have the same steps but is presenting differences concerning amount and quality. I mean terrorism is not an end in itself but a means of exerting political pressure and influence or α power conservation policy. It has taken various forms throughout human history and mankind, but it has not lost its basic characteristic, the exploitation of innocent civilians to serve interests, policies, depending on the prevailing political, social, economic, cultural and religious conditions. Terrorism started to evolve into an international security issue after the decade of '80, and especially after 9/11 with the resurgence of religious fanaticism.

So, one of the main causes of Radicalisation is the globalisation, the modernity - from 1982 till 1989 there were cosmogonic changes in Europe and in the international political arena (the Soviet Union, formerly existing socialism), therefore a morphological differentiation in Europe was a reality: ethnic conflicts, racism resurgence, economies collapse, social conflicts, and delicate political climate.

The dissolution of the Soviet military structures, the illegal sale and trafficking of weapons and systems due to poverty, gaps in power and room for multiple conflicts (like Chechnya, Kashmir, Sri Lanka, Spain, Turkey) facilitated the situation. This globalisation provoked in Muslim countries corrosion in traditions and values, economic, political and cultural turmoil and tension due to great social and economic inequalities. The West has threatened the cultural and religious identity. This sparked extreme ideas, fuelling recruitment movements, which had intended to use terror tactics.

I think about the causes of Radicalisation. For me, an overall strategy addressing the root causes that produce Radicalisation and terrorism must be implemented and fair treatment of universal issues (like poverty, social exclusion and deprivation) with more sensitivity for cultural and religious diversity. I believe Radicalisation being an act that occurs because some organisation or just an individual wants to achieve a goal, is given by the fact that is worst conditions negotiation that could improve a situation. The extremist usually takes refuge in the fact being touched by violence from the other party that fights to justify their own violent action, such as in the case of those terrorist factions fighting against the US and Israel.

While I understand that the problem also is much more difficult because the parties are not very pragmatic and are very loaded with historical, religious and territorial factors that impede be more practical when it comes to obtaining a solution. I see Radicalisation as a tool to recruit people that have been hurt due to some type of loss or feel economic disadvantage because of others. Radicalisation is a process of mind so certainly the most appropriate tool to study it would be psychology. Because there are multiple variables for being unhappy or dissatisfied as well as variables in the way one would respond - so we cannot design a tailor-made solution.

What is more important to understand is that the "perception" of every individual in a terror group is not similar and more important than that is the **"perception" may not be correct at all."** This may be an important factor in the spread and stabilisation of the group. There is no injustice but the idea is floated that there is injustice. Religious thoughts are presented in the manner it never existed.... If we go deeply, we also find that in many instances many state players have played a crucial role in the propagation of the wrong perception.

Addressing this to the Radicalisation of recruits in Western Europe, part of the process has to be to get a French citizen, say, who has never been outside of France to identify with the injustices done to a group of people at a way for geographic, social, cultural distance. The Kouachi Brothers came to believe that injustices were done to "their people," before they stepped outside Paris's suburbs.

Cherif Kouachi had a very strong response to seeing a prisoner mistreated at Abu Ghraib. Both brothers were of Algerian descent but had not grown up Muslim and did not seem to be a part of any traditional culture. Definitely, they already felt a part of a group that the larger society discriminated against. And their own story was riddled with loss. But now that personal narrative, that personal grievance has to be transformed into the narrative of Iraqis, Afghanis, and the people affected by the West's wars. I think Radicalisation must include, for some, a process of re-identification. The question concerning what causes Radicalisation raises an interesting examination about terrorism in various societies. One can argue that the primordial causes of

Radicalisation results from what criminologists would consider as "relative deprivation."

I believe that the need to create a positive self-image is a core psychological need, which motivates many Radicalisation processes. It relates strongly to the idea of a need of significance and the concept of self-enhancement in psychology. Also, the need to belong (belongingness) is also a core psychological need, which motivates Radicalisation, in my view. Another essential psychological need, which motivates Radicalisation, is probably the need for 'deep meaning' (e.g. what is the purpose of my life? Is there an afterlife, and how do I prepare for an afterlife?). Religions and ideologies certainly give individual's material to fulfil these psychological needs. This kind of explanation also explains why well educated and rich people become Radicalised and do suicide mission for their faith? It is crystal clear, that Radicalisation is not simply because of social or economic problems.

It would appear that people can enter the process of Radicalisation/ become Radicalised for all manner of reasons, however, the most common reasons are fundamentally based on the most widespread problems in society, i.e. issues regarding religious beliefs, nationalism, ethnicity, social standing, economics, etc. I believe that these "larger", more widespread issues are the main causes because these are what is reported on most frequently and would generally be the promoted motivation behind the terrorist group activities, however the reasons behind lone wolf actions can be deeply personal to that individual, while recognising that there are more common, there are potentially as many reasons for Radicalisation as there are reasons for grievance. Radicalisation is based on an individual's choice to uphold and stand for a belief contrary to that of the societal norm.

It does not matter if that belief is based on religion, science, or culture the overall differing of opinion with the societal norm is what makes an individual 'radical'.

There are a few examples of eco-terrorist groups in the United States. These people commit acts that - while rarely do they result in injuries to individuals - could ultimately result in the death of others. They hold a radical belief that animals should be free to live in the wild, unmolested by the touch of mankind. This is an unpopular belief because the results of this would have a drastic impact on the daily lives of many Americans. Animal products, testing and the results of experiments in which animals, as used, has a significant impact on the products we use in our daily lives. Thus, these animal rights groups which are willing to resort to property damage, even to the extent of blowing up facilities and offices of companies participating in such acts, are essentially committing acts of terror for the cause in which they believe. They have become Radicalised in their beliefs that they are willing to commit violent acts in order to further their beliefs and ideology. Radicalisation could happen due to many known and unknown reasons. As every individual has a different level of mental approaches about any subject/situation. The basic reasons experts say for becoming a Radicalised individual are; Personal issues, religious extremism, political reasons, ethnic reasons, psychological reasons, sense of being abandoned in society and or lack of basic resources like food, shelter and health etc.

There are two kinds of people, one who in case of poverty or problem tries to find the solution and the other kind of people who of course are mentally weak tries to blame others for their grievances. Even if in some cases the latter kind is right in their thinking, but this does not permit them to be Radicalised and do nasty works for the satisfaction of their conscience. Basic social awareness and education could play a vital role in stopping individuals from being Radicalised. It is a responsibility of the state/government to initiate such programs for the welfare of the state and society.

The ideology behind terrorist activity need to be understood carefully, critically and from a different perspective because without understanding the ideology -root cause then proffering counter Radicalisation would be a problem. It is interesting to note that in De-Radicalisation process, the power of persuasion is more important than **stating facts** when trying to win a superior argument. I think understanding ideology is vital! Ideology like Radicalisation begins with the individual and sprouts within groups. Groups have an ideology if one would accept the fact that individuals do. However, if one does not believe ideology exists within individuals, then naturally it does not exist within groups. Ideology springs from belief systems. How does belief system form? Values, customs, environment, religious/political indoctrinations, etc... I can state with some degree of credibility that one has a belief system.

Radicalisation and Belief System

What has formed that belief system is a good research question? How does that belief system help or hinder the Radicalisation process? It does not occur within a vacuum. It's like a tree. The single seed grows and builds roots, flourishes and if not cut back (trimmed) may become so large that it prevents anything to grow and flourish underneath it until the limbs begin to break off and the light finally reaches the ground. Ideology plays a part in Radicalisation, for sure, but ideology comes as a result of perceived or real injustice. Ideology is born out of these injustices and again it depends on the ideology. I don't think it is overstated at all since terrorist groups or lone wolves share the same ideas or desire to change. Without ideology, the use of violence would be just an act of crime, or insanity, without any specific purpose.

But the mere presence of ideology, in this particular case, a radical thinker, doesn't make him or her engage in violent behaviour. "Ideologies are specific belief systems that interpret grievances or interpret the world around them like so, assigns blame for the things that are wrong in the world, provides a vision for how that world should be, and most importantly tells an individual what they can do or what they need to do."

"Without ideology, the use of violence would be just an act of crime...without any specific purpose." It is the ideology that fuels that Radicalisation. The individuals in question, do not comprehend how complex the world is. They do not see the grey areas in the society in which they live. They don't ask why their government makes the decisions that it does, they simply know that decisions are made, they do not agree with these decisions, and they want to change them rather than try to understand them. They then allow these beliefs to outline their course of action and be the source of their violence. In my personal opinion, calling ideology a "frame" is a very good way to express that it is what sets a limit and defines the level of terrorism. I think ideology is not under-stated and shouldn't be underestimated in the future, as it is a very important element of Radicalisation. A specific belief system can determine the vision of a group and tell the individuals what to do and do not. Ideology polarises society, defines the parameters of violence and shapes propaganda.

I think, what could help to decrease the number of terrorists is, to prevent the individuals to meet this ideology.

These visions tend to be very attractive, desirable and they promise a lot of things or individuals who struggle from grievance, depression, loss of status or honour. As they are simplified their persuasive force is quite high. Therefore, it is very hard to compete with them. But I think once an individual can look at them rationally, and they are more informed about the background of the ideology (they often lack a proper background) they will be less likely to identify themselves with such visions and join a terrorist group. But it would be a long and difficult process as terrorist groups have their own ways to spread their message and they can easily find the right target audience.

There is no person, group of person or organisation without ideology. If you personally don't like one or two things that are generally accepted and it's a norm in the society, at that point you have "framed" for yourself an ideology. This new attitude or belief that will be at variance with the general belief of others would always clash whenever it comes in collision with that which is generally accepted. More often than not, the minority "believe" will desire to seek for faithful to support his ideology and spread it beyond his door post, in other to have his kind here and there. In most cases, he succeeds to go beyond a city, nation and our continent. When that has been achieved, the minority group would be regarded as a fanatic, extremist and so on. To stop further spread of anti-human ideologies in today's world, nations should have legislative framework that regulates, faith and believes, to mitigate the rising of fanaticism and extremism in the world.

In Nigeria Boko Haram initially anchored their grievances on the existence of western education in the country. While they condemned western education, they use the western education apparatuses to communicate with one another and advance their ideologies. Ideologies are not only peculiar to terrorist groups. Individuals do initiate ideologies. When an anti-human ideology is allowed to spread it runs in a parallel line to societal norms and values. The government should always nip all anti-societal ideology on the bud. Terrorist groups exist all over the world already, what is left to do is for the unfortunate country to fight it. To prevent the pluralism of terrorist groups in a country, the government should always try its best to assuage the grievances of its citizens less it swells up and runs out of control Ideology and Radicalisation go almost hand-in-hand. But I think, it is also important to focus on the targets of persuasion, the people who the radical orator/group wishes to convert and recruit. I think in many cases they take advantage of people's social situation.

These indoctrinated veterans leave their area to export their beliefs and tactic and targeting practices to places where there is already some sort of conflict.

We may assume that the people who live in a conflict area are living under difficult conditions and probably have been and are still treated unequally to others. Here we could associate it with personal and community grievance: these people feel like wrong is being caused to them or to their community and they wish to change it.

Ideology plays a part in Radicalisation, for sure, but ideology comes as a result of perceived or real injustice. Ideology is born out of these injustices. So, if that is true, then perhaps as societies and as governments, we need to proactively address the perceived injustice, if possible, at least to build bridges through listening, having empathy, trying to find some common ground. I realize this may be simplistic, but it seems we never really want to tackle the roots of the problems, but merely the symptoms of the problems.

Ethnic Discrimination Leads Radicalism

There is another great factor associated with a social norm is ethnic discrimination. Ekaterina Stepanova wrote in her research paper "research shows that terrorism is most closely connected to political factors and conditions such as chronic discrimination, including discrimination on an ethnic basis or the violations or absence of civil and political rights." For example the LTTE in Sri Lanka arose out of the Tamil people's frustration as a result of real injustice to them as the minority people. The Rajapaksa government, instead of addressing the injustice in a fair and equitable way, they waged a war against the LTTE and the LTTE was trounced. Symptom squashed.

There was hope with the new president in Sri Lanka, that the injustices and inequalities levelled at the Tamil people under the Rajapaksa government will be addressed. Otherwise, the LTTE will rise again, perhaps in a new form, but it will resurrect, driven by a new ideology. An Ideology is a key aspect of Radicalisation. If people are being humiliated, and they feel that the world is against them and there is a charismatic figure who presents a set of beliefs about how the world should really look like and insist on presenting violence as the only means left to achieve the real world outcome, then it's only a matter of time until people mobilize to take action and I don't think all of them are joining different groups for the same reasons, I mean, yes there may be a common view for all -that they have been mistreated by the U.S for example, but some of them wants revenge, others want money or power or resources and so on, but as long as there is a general common ground for all of them it would be easy to radicalise all together.

For instance, at the end of the World War I, some of the European states started to feel sorry for the sanctions imposed against Germany because they were too harsh, not to mention that the European states make it look like Germany was the only state responsible for the war. Hitler who felt humiliated broke all the treaties and started its own plan, presenting people how badly they were treated and that they deserved better and that they could do better and German people supported him. Hitler realised his influence which he wanted to turn in to radicalise the nation, he moved on with its ideology that German's blood is the purest blood. Hitler said in his book Mein Kampf that **"God started a project (the world) but God forgot to finish it and this is why we can't see God because someone else has to finish His "project" that is to kill Jews"**. Therefore, I believe that ideology- a set of beliefs that describe the world both what's wrong and how should the world look like, plays a very important role in Radicalisation ... the worst part comes when a charismatic figure manages to achieve people's support for an awful cause...

The ideology plays an important role in the Radicalisation process, mainly because sometimes it erases the possibility of an alternative answer to the comprehension of a determinate problem (the black and White effect). However, I think, we might take care in order to suggest in which sense ideology is so degenerative that leads to misconceptions of the world. An ideology is a set of conscious or unconscious ideas which constitute one's goals, expectations, and actions and it's a way of looking at things. Basically, having different views or not accepting what other members of society do. Also, when I did more research in regards of Radicalisation process, I found this very interesting how different studies show that some people actually believed that terrorist may have mental illness problems or lower educational status because of the acts they are committing normal human beings would not commit such 'evil' things. But recent research shows that it is not the case the percentage of mental illness is about the same if not lower than average citizen or the general population as a whole. The key thing to understand here is actually as a terrorist group they want to develop that commitment to violence and willing to commit those horrible acts against humanity.

Global Caliphatic Ideology

An ideology is a very powerful starting point. It is engrained in us to stand up for our beliefs. Therefore, it is indeed a fertile ground for radicalisation to grow in whatever process it follows, ideology remains the purpose upon which individual can always fall back on when in doubt. I think that not only is it an important starting point but it is Aldo a dud raining point. It is also based on this that they might get public support and sympathy.

While it is true that ideology plays a foundational role in grooming future terrorists, the mechanism for Radicalisation varies from individual to individual- and even from group to group.

For example, if we examine the "pious movements" of Islam, which has been attempting to restore the Caliphate, we will soon come to realise, despite a general consensus on ideology to re-establish the Caliphate, in group divisions exist regarding strategies of implementation- due to what has been characterised as "collective identity." "Pious zealots" might choose Jihadist methods to restore the Caliphate based on their own group specific grievance with governing environs in their society.

If we examine the context of the Caliphate original ideology, from a purely religious standpoint, without the association of violent actors and terrorism, we see the similarity with Christendom aspirations and already existing form of Christendom governance. One can assume, without the Jihadist desire to impose their extremist beliefs, a Caliphate scenario would be just like the Christians having a single religious entity called the Vatican, in Rome with a Pope as the head. The fact is, all Christians do not submit to Vatican ideology and teachings- but neither does the Vatican impose or compel its religious values on others, as we are seeing in the case of these Jihadists and overzealous pious advocates, for the return of the Caliphate. Our responsibility is to learn more about the underlying causes that motivate terrorism in each society, further exploring the mechanism of the "two pyramids theory" (opinion pyramid and action pyramid) instead of the weak blabbing we constantly see on network televisions, where Islamic and/or Muslims ideology are branded and blame for terrorism. The right-wing ideology strongly exists in Europe; here I provide the example of the far-right rally in Germany against the anti-Islam.

That arguments and facts are not working, is currently visible in Germany among the followers of "Pegida" - an anti-Islam/far-right movement which has attracted an increasing number of people during the last weeks. The movement has its majority of followers in a part of Germany where there are the fewest migrants and Muslims. Some extremists use the grievances of ordinary people and their fear to be lost in an increasingly complex world by assigning the blame on Muslims/ immigrants and use the mentioned black and white simplifications for current problems in the society which might be neglected by the political parties.

There is a difference between the two, especially in the US context. All terrorists are extremists but not all extremists are terrorists. My understanding is that it is a movement with strong right-wing extremist participation. I haven't seen any evidence that they are connected to a terrorist group which uses violence "outside the context of legitimate warfare permitted by International Humanitarian Law." Do they have a well -defined ideology or just a racist anti-immigration and anti-Muslim agenda? Are their grievances economic primarily -- in the East as you well know there's far more unemployment, lower standards of living etc? Do they have psychological grievances like loss of ethnic and religious identity?

Here I highlight the answer, to weaken an extremist ideology governments and societies take a multi-pronged approach to address the grievances, counter ideology and provide safe identity. What would it take for this group to progress to violence? If we look at the Radicalisation Opinion Pyramid it seems that they are sympathisers but have not yet framed a cause to support. However, if the shaming/humiliation that Annett Shabani reports continues there could quite easily be a consolidation of views leading to the formation of a "cause" with its own ideology. In the hands of an accomplished recruiter, it's quite possible that this group could become a real threat. The Pegida has two options open either it turns to the most violent group turn into a terrorist group, could turn into a political party in the line of the French far-right party Front National. By the way, Pegida has just spread to another country, The UK & Austria, where it organized rallies. These movements and parties indicate this phenomenon does not circumscribe only to Germany.

The Ideology is bred into the individual. We are social creatures, long ago accepting the advantage of the group over the individual and reinforced through millions of years of evolution. Acceptance into the group is absolutely necessary and conformity is required. Even those few who will say they do not conform. During the heady days of the Cold War, the communist/capitalist rhetoric flew often, two separate ideologies both struggling to 'save' the world.

And while the style of governments may have differed, the average American and the average Soviet citizen were very similar and wanted the same things. The difference was only in what they were taught about the primacy of their culture over others. The battle is necessary - my group is better than your group because it is my group and an extension of me. If the group fails, then I will fail. If I fail, I may die. Therefore, my group is better than yours.

Groups (cultures) can live harmoniously, with a set of rules in place, but those rules will only remain as long as both groups do not feel threatened. Samuel Huntington's Clash of Civilisations does a much better job explaining this than I. Terrorists do not start as terrorists, they begin with a gripe, a complaint, an unfairness they feel must be resolved. This is the Grievance portion of the four-step Radicalisation process. It is because of their culture, upbringing, teachings that they feel this grievance exists.

If we recognise this grievance early enough, we can stem the tide of terrorism by treating the cause and not the symptom. For all of our talk of defeating terrorism, we are fighting it too late in the process. We all believe one branch is the best (e.g. the army is better than the air force). But then even within a single branch, we break it down further - my trade is better than yours because the infantry does the hard work; my unit is better than yours because we travel by mechanised vehicles; my company is better than yours because we are led by x-commander; my platoon is better than yours because (we carry the heavy machine guns'/grenade launchers, have the lowest casualty rate, etc). And all of this comes from the ideology - a set of beliefs of what is wrong and what it should be and blueprints for action. Ideology definitely seems to be a key factor in Radicalisation. However, I think all of the components have their equal value because one cannot just develop ideology with having reason to change their beliefs in the first place.

They would require something wrong to be righted (grievance) and to be able to be influenced (cognitive opening). To counter a lack of tolerance, I believe, requires education and the ability to learn about other viewpoints.

Believe or Die

Western thought and philosophy are based on reason. Religion is simply not. Religion is based upon passion, the antithesis of reason. It is like saying "My invisible friend is better than your invisible friend. Prove to me that he is not." Education to extremist groups, be they Islamic or Christian or Jews, is to recite the Book as the Word of God. Are we as mere humans going to reason with God? If you, as a Christian, do not follow the Ten Commandments to the letter, you are violating God's Laws as given to Moses. If a Muslim does not follow the Quran to the letter as given to the Prophet Muhammad, then that person is violating God's Law.

How can I educate my way around those viewpoints, especially when the person that I am educating says "You must *believe* what I *believe* or die?" Ideology is one of the four characteristics of Radicalisation. It is a set of beliefs that describes what is wrong with the world and what the world should be. It takes place in sequential order- polarisation, Radicalisation of recruits and mobilisation towards violence. The potency of ideology in the Radicalisation process is captured vividly in the quote from Black Tamil Tiger's videos, mention is the report "Family and relationships are forgotten in that place. There was no place for love. That means a passion and loyalty to that group, to those who sacrificed their lives for the group. Then I came to a stage where I had no love for myself. I had no value for my life. I was ready to give myself fully, even to destroy myself fully, and in order to destroy another".

I am convinced that getting to the root of the Radicalisation process by making it difficult for terrorists to recruit people will go a long way in countering terrorism. What motivates someone to actively support the advocates of extreme Islamist ideology? What motivates someone to be a terrorist or a martyr? How an ideology which is supportive of violent Islamist extremism is going to influence people, in order to support the commission of terrorist acts? Which are the factors associated with a particular ideology that would eventually lead to violent Islamist extremism? The Radicalisation and recruitment of civilians and the assistance in war zones is not a new phenomenon and this can be seen in religious, political, social and psychological perspective. But every attempt of interpretation can present significant limitations as the reasons that trigger someone to become an extremist "jihadist" or something else differ from person to person. The ideological framework of the Islamic State in conjunction with the successes in the field of battle is considered by many analysts as an inspiration. The extremist ideology will prove attractive to many Muslims. Maybe ideology is proven as the main source for the Radicalisation of potential supporters of Al Qaeda and other Islamic terrorist organisations around the world, but I believe mostly in the role of personality - terrorism is not triggered only by ideology but by the individual personality and life impressions too, that there is imminent danger from the society in which he/ she lives. Ideology does not only appear from the void but affects special traits of personality and behaviour consequently only under certain circumstances.

According to my understanding, terrorists are fully aware of the impact of their actions and for this reason, they will need a very strong driving force to help those overcome doubts and moral dilemmas.

Many psychological theories (like Sykes and Matza) are trying to interpret tendencies of people to extreme acts and behaviours, because they put themselves defensively against "evil", whatever is this, considering, therefore, their obligation to achieve "good" through violence. I think most of the terrorists present themselves as fighters, defenders against "evil" because this "evil" threatens their existence, their lives, and their identity.

Bill Braniff of Maryland University states bout the extreme ideology; "ideology incorporates belief systems. It is these belief systems that form the foundation for an individual's world view. Ideology is the incorporation of the values, customs, beliefs that encumbers an individual one way or the other. The attack upon an ideology only strengthens the righteousness of the ideology aka belief system. However, understanding the ideology within the framework of anther's perspective outside one's own perspective is a challenge that is difficult to overcome. However, it is only through walking in their shoes ideologically speaking, can one develop the necessary countermeasures that would dent the wrongness or rightness of the ideology."

I found emphasis of separating ideology from terrorist acts important because many people hold strong political and religious views without performing any type of violent act. However, the depiction of ideology did seem to lack adequate emphasis. In these media reports, the ideology of the terrorists is presented as the reason for brutally murdering innocent people. According to the report published in the wall street journal: "The ideology is not simply editorialising by some members of the media, but presented as direct quotes by the terrorist themselves. Consequently".

I think ideology requires a stronger presentation in the role of the development of a terrorist, especially one who becomes a terrorist in the neighbourhood of other terrorists; i.e. a local person who already shares the basic ideology and culture of the terrorist group. It makes more sense to conduct a psychological profile of a non-native person (such as an American) who lacks the political and religious upbringing of the established terrorists. Many young British today lack any type of strong religious ideology; so, the psychological profile provides the only visible nexus to their action of becoming a terrorist; i.e., the psychology leads the ideology.

It would be quite interesting to read the personal histories of a British who became terrorists, as a way to understand precisely what caused them to change their worldview, assuming they held to a specific worldview prior to their change.

Perhaps there was some type of void in their belief system, to begin with, and the terrorists simply filled the void. I have read hundreds of articles, journals and books on the issue of Radicalisation and De-Radicalisation, attended many events held by national and international organisations but none have produced a concrete solution how to stop people being a Radicalised? How to counter the Radicalised ideology of extremism? Every institute worked and researched on how it emerges, how to produce or how to spread and what are the causes behind grown up this ideology but none have introduced any final solution against this virus. I must mention one thing that every master of this field would agree on that Radicalisation is the process of the psychological norm. It's a total mind process system. One could assess this system through education and theoretical way, but cannot contract to damage it because to counter the Radicalisation; it must introduce a mathematical and empirical system to stop the Radicalised process in extremist mind. It is totally a practical process. Do not forget that there are many shapes of Radicalisation, few I mention here. 1- Right wing Radicalisation 2- Left wing Radicalisation 3- Ethno- national Radicalisation 4- Religious Radicalisation I introduce one new system of Radicalisation which I call: 5- Crime based Radicalisation.

First 4 shapes of Radicalisation are very well known in the world through the educational system and these all 4 shapes of Radicalisation are being educated in universities and academic institutes but last 5th one Crime Based Radicalisation is not very well known but only present in very small areas of study or research. We should not forget that the process of Radicalisation goes through the mind psychologically, hence we treat and deal with every extremist based on psychological process. Crime based Radicalisation motivates someone to commit a crime and there are many reasons behind it. One of the main reasons behind the crime-based Radicalisation is Biological factor. The biological factor is another cause of the crime and in the biological theory. It is stated that criminals are born, not made and that a criminal personality can be inherited from your parents in their genes. Genes might affect the way in which parts of a criminal's brain work. Crime is simply not a static; universal things need no explanation in itself. According to famous psychologist McGuire:

"There are no acts that can be called a crime. Crime is not a distinct type of behaviour. For example, something you have taken without the permission of the owner it is not called crime sometimes or killing another person sometimes is not a crime. You may kill someone for your self-defence or it could be accidentally likewise using drugs is a crime in one country but legally allowed in another country. In every society, there are different social constructions and values. In most societies lying, stealing, violence etc. behaviours are unacceptable."

The crime-based radicalisation is being treated by the criminal psychologists likewise religious could be treated by either same criminal psychologists or Religious psychologists.

Secular and Religious Radicalisation

Perhaps the Radicalisation process and the rivalries are due to tragic socio-economic circumstances and ideological differences, but terrorism can flourish on the basis of any extreme ideology, religion or cultural/ value system. The degree of fanaticism has changed, so I can say that there must be some differences in process concerning techniques of proselytism, recruitment, and psychological strategies of persuasion, oppressive methods for inserting in a group, maybe bodily strategies of persuasion, compulsive actions, mystic treatment, and confession. Unlike secular terrorists, those who are inspired by religion, they consider "blind" violence as morally justified and imperative for achieving its objectives. For the religious terrorist, violence is a sacred duty, for persons from religion are necessary to bless terrorist operations before they are performed. Religion here is a legitimising force, as conveyed by scripture or by a representative of the sulphur. Religious violence is more pernicious than the political violence due to legality values and righteousness and the concept of morality, which is influencing and persuading the terrorist.

The legalised violence in the eyes of God that neither civilians nor innocent citizens are figuring and the high degree of fanaticism, as perceived by extremist terrorists, are not distinguishing innocent people because the ultimate goal is served. Religiously inspired terrorists are seeking religious justifications for violence against anyone opposed to their faith. Secular ideology is the separation of government from religion. It involves asserting the right to be free from religious rule and teachings. It is pluralistic, tolerant and has deep respect for individuals, equality of all people and the right to actualise their aspirations. Religion does not have an economic or political objective, but a humane objective. However, it becomes a religious ideology, when it deceptively takes advantage of people's religious allegiances, to put it into action, its ideological beliefs, through Radicalisation.

Secular Radicalisation seems borne from social injustice, then there is a formation of an ideology to combat the injustice followed by a systematic methodology of propaganda to recruit supporters. In religious Radicalisation, an ideology is already in place. Although they may start the same, I believe secular and religious ideologies have their differences. People being wronged by their government may hold the ideology that they should overthrow the government and make a change because they are being mistreated by their government. A religious ideology of the same situation may have stronger influence because the people are being wronged and this is not how God intended it to be.

Now the matter is this, if it is correct that the psychological profile is the reason for an individual to become a terrorist, then it follows that the type of terrorism, type of ideology, whether secular or religious does not matter. Because the individual's psychological make-up was already predisposed to becoming some type of, or any type of terrorist.

However, I think a formative young person would tend to lean towards the political or religious view of the terrorist community in his area of residence. The scenario of an American who becomes influenced by overseas terrorists may be somewhat different in nature, as the American still has the ability to pick and choose his ideology or secular terrorist philosophy du jour, as he pleases. A young person living in a third world nation who is constantly exposed to a particular political or religious view may not have much choice, especially if the views are enforced with the threat of violence. It may not matter much if the terrorist philosophy is political or religious, in that regard, as the threat of violence would enforce the individual to toe the line to that view. It perhaps raises the rhetorical question: do all terrorists sincerely want to be terrorists? Or are some of them (rank-and-file, I am not referring to the leadership), coerced to play the parts they play?

In fact, an ideally of the Radicalisation process seem to be the same either in a secular or religious situation. Grievance plays a big role, this means there has to be a pressing need for Radicalisation to take root, for example, Islamist decry the debauchery in Christianity and other religions.

They justify their actions as a way to cleanse the earth of infidels as they claim. On the secular side, the advocates tend to state that it is because of exploitation or being impoverished or side-lined in the government, for example, the FARC and LTTE. Ideology also is significant because it entails indoctrination to create a belief system and sense of belonging to the cause at hand hence making Radicalisation easier. In a religious sense, there is the creation of intolerance towards other faiths while promoting the one advocated for. Secular the actors also tend to reinforce their ideologies and step up their activities based on such beliefs. For example, extreme environmentalists or ECO terrorists who bomb or even perpetrate other forms of violence to state their cause. The Radicalisation process is similar for secular and religious ideologies.

Both are groups of people who strongly believe in what they are trying to accomplish. These groups may go about their ideology in different ways but they start off in the same fashion as both groups feel they have a grievance and grow from there. Groups on both sides have joined violent and nonviolent causes to further their ideology, the interesting study is when the groups feel they must become violent and to what extent that violence must occur.

It seems that way. If you apply either the NYPD's Radicalisation steps, or the "Staircase to Terrorism" by F. Moghaddam, it doesn't seem to matter what the particular ideology is, all that matters is that a group or individual is aggrieved, confirms their biases with information (usually from the web nowadays, but passing around holy books or underground literature has the same effect), finds a "leader" figure who gives them motive and channels the anger, and then, leads them to use the tools of terror (fear, violence). You can apply this rubric to state-sponsored terror--even a rudimentary study of right-wing, radical groups in Weimar Germany shows how you can get the Nazi's. Or for another German example, how the Red Army Faction grew in West Germany (RAF being socialist guerrillas).

Secular vs Religious Ideology

Now if someone raises the question "Radicalisation processes are different for secular versus religious ideologies?" my answer would be "No" the same process is followed regardless of the type of information or propaganda used to get to the desired goal. The secular terrorist still believes that they are righting a wrong. They are still attempting to achieve that self-importance, that sense of mattering in the world that the religious terrorist believes. The religious terrorist only ties what they perceive to be the word of god or the word of a prophet to their acts to bring justification to their cause. Everyone who is Radicalised, whether this is regarding animal welfare, left-wing ideology, right-wing ideology, environmentalism, you name it all seem to share the same sorts of convictions. As I mentioned earlier, it is the ideology that matters, which is why it is arguable that religious motivation is secular and the secular motivation is religious. They all share the same characteristics in a black and white worldview, the sense of urgency and the belief in an exclusive knowledge not shared by the majority of the populace.

This no doubt makes the recipient of this knowledge feel special and reinforces the commitment to the group, whatever the underlying cause. Obviously, this has something to do with the reward and loyalty centres of the brains of those affected (not that there is anything abnormal in this, the results clearly fall within the standard spectrum of attachments, the only outliers occur in how far people are prepared to go to "right the wrong".

I don't feel like there is much different in the process by which the Radicalisation takes place. There are four components evident in the Radicalisation process. Grievance, cognitive opening, ideology, and mobilisation. I believe that, in some capacity, both secular and religious groups go through relatively the same process. They both possess, in some varying fashion, these four components. The difference between the two is the ideology that fuels their actions. Obviously, with religious groups, they are directed by their religious teachings. They believe that they are doing as their God wills. Secular groups, though, aren't going to be directed by the belief in a higher being, but rather in more of a belief in social conviction.

Secular movements proposing concrete goals provide also milestones for their achievement ("convince the masses", "stop this or that policy", "topple the government" and "establish a new guidance"). Thus, when one is not implemented, the conviction of the follower and his/her drive to act can be jeopardised. Religious movements, being based on immaterial notions and usually providing less precise objectives-though they can also be politically based, cf. Muslim Brotherhood- are less prone to a comparison between the goals and achievements. "Re-establish the khalifate", "Destroy the Western Shaitan (Devil)", "Establish the Shari'a" are very distant, not to be achieved in one's lifetime goals. Moreover, the progress toward their realisation cannot be concretely measured. Therefore, the follower of such a doctrine cannot be discouraged by failure, as he/she does not expect complete success. Besides, it's easier to feed him/her with encouraging "events" as he/she cannot compare them to concrete, evaluable milestones. People hold their religious views more tightly than political or other secular views and beliefs. I would expect that many people feel they were born into a religion, just as I feel that I was born Muslim because both of my parents and their ancestors are Muslims, and I grew up in a Muslim society. We have seen the political, environmental, and social landscape change, sometimes quickly and frequently, but overall, religion remains fairly constant therefore making it an easy ground to target and radicalise someone on.

Radicalisation Processes

Radicalisation processes are no different for secular than for religious ideologies. The process itself is a roadmap where different specialized individuals step by step, manoeuvre and seemingly guide the handpicked target individual towards the different milestones, the milestones are always flexible in time. The grip gets firmer and firmer parallel with that the control of the target individuals mind do too. To speed up the process they use any tool available; high tech, IT, Apps and even isolation.

It has an impact on how antagonism appears. But the kind of Radicalisation we're talking about in terrorism leading up to becoming a Jihadist is the kind that ends up in an emotionless state that murders strategically and in cold blood. No terrorist organisation would use someone emotionally involved for personal emotional reasons. However, that may be how the process of segregating the potential individual begins. The selecting process is made from out of the genetic ability for the aimed mission. If not, they would most likely never succeed. Regardless of how devoted and convinced, not all can become that Radicalised and in fact some simply can't become Radicalised at all. Whatever brainwash, torture or mind controlling technique is being used. We must always remember that there is a difference between being a fundamentalist and being a murdering extremist who don't regard people of other ideologies worthy of having a life.

With someone's particular set of Christian beliefs, to see anti-abortion violence described as "terrorism" resonates with him in a way that for example discussions of the IRA's activity and motives don't. As we were discussing elsewhere the latter has a very large social and historical component besides the religious affiliation. Anti-abortion violence, on the other hand, is very recent and they are almost entirely based on religious ideas Thinking about anti-abortion violence being defined as terrorism helps us to feel more clearly how people in other societies encountering different "terrorist" ideologies can have levels of support for them as they match their own views and beliefs.

Discrimination is one of the main tools dragging people into violent extremism. Those who aren't socialist or those who are a different type of atheism are being discriminated... just like the Nazis... Nazis discriminated Jews and they killed everyone who were helping Jews, so they discriminated almost everybody who was not sharing Hitler's ideas- following the expression: "either you are with me or against me (which makes you my enemy)". However, the comparison between atheists and Nazis is limited there, at discrimination, because actually, Hitler believed in a God in a Higher Power and he said in his book that God didn`t finish its project (the world) and its Hitler`s duty to finish what God started and that is to kill Jews. Not only he did believe in a supreme power but he also saw himself as a half/semi-God. I am still very much impressed even today about how one man`s charisma can mobilise millions of people.

After the Communist revolutions in the USSR and China, and after the French Revolution in France, there were attempts with varying success to remove religion completely from the states. The leaders of these revolutions were not campaigning as atheists, they had different main ideas, but atheism was a part of their ideologies and so they attempted to implement it.

The Radicalisation process is the same regardless. Taking it a step further, Radicalisation is the same regardless of whether the cause is unjust or just, in the eyes of the viewer. Radicals are idealists, they are the ones who see the cause as all important believe the ends will justify the means...the greater good. Consider the communist/capitalist debates prevalent throughout the Cold War. Both ideologies had believers with as much fervour for their view as any religion. The connecting issue to it all is that belief in a higher purpose of power. In religion, it is an anthropomorphised god handcrafted to fit into a culture. With democracy, it is the belief that we must all work towards a time when we are all 'free'.

In my opinion, that's the best way to see tendencies for Radicalisation in a school, at work or in our relationships. It makes it easier to detect even tendencies in teens early on but it is also important that we can never change another person. However, we can counteract in trying to trigger instincts that will set for young teens and other people who are being misled back on track before it is too late.

Religion is something that strikes at the very core of our being. For very religious people, their religion is not a part of their life, it IS their life. Most of us learn religious lessons at a very young age when they have no ability to make distinctions between fact and belief. Some people begin to shed their beliefs as they grow older. For others, it becomes a deeply ingrained way of being. Although many religions teach tolerance, they all profess that their beliefs are "right" or at least "more right" than others. For deeply religious people, their religion is tightly bound to the sense of who they are and, therefore, dictates many, if not most, of their daily behaviours. Religious beliefs can be a source of great good. The deeply religious are often more involved in volunteer work to help others, but for a very small group of people this sense of "being right" can become twisted into allowing all sorts of negative actions. For example, the anti-abortionists (the Christian right) mentioned above can mentally justify murdering doctors who perform abortions because the anti-abortionists believe the doctors are committing murder. It doesn't matter that abortion is legal in the US, and that, therefore, the doctors are not committing a crime. The religiously held beliefs of the anti-abortionists supersede the laws of the country they are in and they feel compelled to support what they perceive to be their god's law.

Muslim extremists have committed all kinds of atrocities in the name of Allah. And, although it has been fairly quiet and out of the news for a long time, the conflict between Ireland and the UK used the differences between Catholics and Protestants to fuel the fire. So, I believe that it is possible for people to radicalise along either secular or religious lines, but religion is an especially convenient way to create an "us-versus-them" mentality that takes advantage of already deeply held beliefs. For the Nazis, their politics is the equivalent or even superior to the status of a religion and it was the same with Communism in the former Soviet Union and Mao's China. In Sweden, all children became members in the church by birth. Even children born to parents of other religions. Nowadays, I believe parents can choose upon the birth of a child but that is if they know about it. From an overall counter terrorism perspective that is something to be aware of when we travel from one country to another and when we send our children to schools abroad. Especially since the Radicalisation often sneaks up on the individuals in all societies.

Chapter 2

Global Jihadism

Jihad, Al Qaeda and Radicalisation

Radicalisation is a specific process by which a man or women, old and young, or groups decide to adopt extreme religious or sectarian ideas and aspirations which: (1) reject the status quo; (2) undermine contemporary ideas. Radicalisation by developing an extremist way of life and ideology which justify violence is one possible pathway into terrorism involvement but it is certainly not the only one. The United States Counterterrorism Centre, in its recent report, noted that the grievance that fuel Radicalisation is diverse and vary across locations and groups. Radicalisation, according to the US Counterterrorism report, is driven by personal concerns at the local level in addition to frustration with international events. In a Netherlands Institute of International Relations recent report, Veldhuis and Staun have broadly defined Radicalisation: "Although radicalisation has increasingly been subjected to scientific studies, a universally accepted definition of the concept is still to be developed".

Nevertheless, faced with pressure to tackle radicalisation, policymakers have developed a few definitions. Definitions of radicalisation most often centre around two different foci: (1) on violent radicalisation, where emphasis is put on the active pursuit or acceptance of the use of violence to attain the stated goal, and (2) on a broader sense of radicalisation, where emphasis is placed on the active pursuit or acceptance of far-reaching changes in

50

society, which may or may not constitute a danger to democracy and may or may not involve the threat of or use of violence to attain the stated goals."

The question is, does the hate come before or after the Radicalisation? Do all those Radicalised even know what it is they are getting Radicalised to? I think answers would also depend on how far or distant one is and has been from the conflicts which seem to give rise to the terrorist groups. I do wish, we could find some individual psychological profiles to isolate that determines susceptibility to Radicalisation and then, more importantly, the move on to mobilisation joining a group like ISIS. But I don't know that there is such a universal personality attribute, attitude, and world-view.

Hatred is certainly a motivator for all kinds of acts and terrorism would appear to be high on the list.

Again, at what point does a Radicalised person feel enough hatred to torture another person, for instance? America endorsed torture as a method for getting information post-9/11—was that hatred operating? Was that revenge? Was that simply a goal-oriented response? Did we cede our civilised instincts to our need for self-preservation? However, Israel's method of getting information is different than the US because Israel does not use any form of torture. Torture is prohibited in Israel by the order of the Supreme Court.

Extreme Islamic Ideology Vs Moderate Islamic Ideology

Islam and Islamism are totally different systems of the world. Islamism is an extreme ideological system and in the democratic society, you could find many ideologies which are operating in different shapes, names and organisational networks in the universe.

Extremism is a strong and most powerful ideology and no any state can counter, control or defeat that ideology. If states try to use force to destroy the Extreme ideology, it will become stronger and if they let it go, it will cause more danger to the nations and to the democratic systems of the world. This ideology is present in every country, especially in Muslim countries. Those who are influenced and adapted by this most dangerous ideology; cannot accept the democratic or Islamic sultanate systems. There is a democratic system in most of the Islamic countries, but some have a sultanate system. Extreme ideology rejects both systems in the world and tries to stabilize their own empire, which surely founded by their so-called ideological fanatics. Moderate Islamic Ideology and Extreme Islamic ideology are two different and opposite ideologies based on totally separate systems which goes against each other.

There is only one solution that can stop and change the extreme Islamic ideology to a moderate and balanced Islamic ideology, which is; to create a stronger ideology that could counter and destroy an extreme ideology. This is not an easy mission as to say, it needs more work, more time, more knowledge, more capabilities and dynamic system that create a new strong ideology against the current extreme ideology. Islamic extreme Ideology is based on religion, no doubt, but the name of Islam has been hijacked by the extremists who manipulated the true face of Islam and mixed with their own extreme ideology and presented it to the world and try to force them to accept it.

The moderate Islamic Ideology still based on religion, the true religion of Islam to counter the extreme ideology. These both ideologies are still fighting each other and trying very hard to destroy one another, but states should support moderate Islamic Ideology by recruiting those Muslim scholars who have vast knowledge of true peaceful Islam and they would be capable to damage the extreme ideology by countering them through their positive knowledge of the moderate face of Islam.

An Ideology can defeat the ideology only, but it depends whose motives and objectives are stronger.

South Asian Islamic extreme ideology was developed in Afghan-Soviet war when Pakistani Intelligence Service (ISI) created extremists and induced violence and extreme Ideology to combat the most powerful Soviet Empire with the help of western powers. Soviet Empire was formed on an ideology too, which called Communism. Communism was a strong and rapidly growing ideology in the world and it was a direct threat to the world's western democratic systems. Western powers needed to destroy this powerful ideology so another strong ideology was created to completely damage the Communist Ideology. Islamic Extreme ideology was formed in the name of religion and that ideology was much more capable and strong ideology than the ideology of Communism. Within eleven years war between two strong ideologies, one old and powerful ideology of Communism with the latest technology was fallen in the hands of newly risen Islamic extreme ideology with the help of Pakistani Intelligence and the western intelligence agencies.

Ideology is a kind of virus, if let it go, it will still grow and if treated it wrongly; it will destroy the entire system. If you counter or destroy the negative virus you have to create a new strong positive virus that can completely vanish the virus that could cause danger to the system. To destroy the Islamic extreme ideology, we have to create another new strong and capable ideology.

According to the Clarion Project "Islamic extreme Ideology can only be countered by undermining the ideology itself. Reformist Muslims that support an interpretation of Islam that is favourable to modernity and Western democracy are viewed as critical to fighting Islamic extremists. Islamic extremism derives from a radical interpretation of Islam. Even among Islamic extremists, there are interpretative differences stemming from different sects and/or doctrines. It's important to note that not all Muslims subscribe to a radical interpretation of Islam. In the West, Islamic extremist groups and their supporters spread their ideology (and, in some cases, directly sponsor terrorism) using a network of front groups. An example would be the Iranian government's use of the Alavi Foundation in New York or the Muslim Brotherhood's establishment of various political organisations under different names." Hatred and extremism are two different ideologies, but in fact, hatred is a sub ideological category of extremism. There is a direct connection between hate, violence and extremism. Extremism and violent extremism are totally different phenomena but are connected to each other because their root causes are the same. The question is this; when does someone become violent extremist?

The answer is simple when he adapts extremism; he first embraces hatred because without hatred you cannot become violent. Once an extremist embrace hatred he automatically jumped on the next stage of extreme ideology which calls violent extremism and violent extremism makes him a violent individual. So, you cannot become violent if you don't have violent behavioural character and that character embrace the behaviour of hate towards the opposite community, nation or religion. Before the terrorist commits terrorist act, he holds three characters with his attitude.

1. Hateful character

2. Extreme ideology

3. Violent behaviour

Once he graduates of all 3 characters, his next step is to cause damage to the opposite community and a system through his actions because terrorist fully wants to generate fear with the opposite population. Terrorism is like violence, disease and natural disasters. It is part of the human condition, but the image of the terrorism, the idea of it; is much more dangerous than the actual physical attack. What we can do is to remove the terror from the terrorism. We need to contain or instinct of fear and hysteria just being aware that the fear is what terrorist really want will help us reduce the impact of an attack. We also need to recognise that even though terrorist does not share our moral values. They are intelligent and their actions are meant to provoke us; it is the response of the population that really reflects the success of the attackers.

This is a very interesting topic which elucidates the basic organisational structure of a terror group. Membership, resources, and organisational structure determine the capabilities of a group reach. A terrorist group operating in accordance motivation by ideology dominated traditional appreciation of terrorism. The structure of a group determines its strengths and weaknesses. The popular image of a group operating according to a specific political agenda and motivated by ideology or the desire for ethnic or national liberation dominated our understanding of terrorism. Terrorist groups may establish cells based on family or employment relationships. These cells are used to control its members. However, with regard to the ideology-based organisations, it aids ideological unity among its members.

Passive supporters may intermingle with active supporters and be unaware of what their actual relationship is to the organisation. Terrorist groups will recruit from populations that are sympathetic to their goals. Religious motivations can also be tied to ethnic and nationalist identities, such as Kashmiri separatists combining their desire to break away from India, a terrorist will evaluate what force protection measures are in effect in the vicinity of a target and determine a cost-benefit analysis.

I entirely focus on the issue of leadership in an organisation as well as the correlation between them. The core of leadership contains power and traits; cognitive, effective, and technical competence overlay the leadership core. The wrong organisational structure might not perform well or may hamper cooperation and thus hinder the completion of orders in due time and within limits of resources and budgets.

Targets, Weapons and Tactics

Most if not all terrorist organisations cannot wage a conventional war against the state or governments. There is a high level of organisation in each of the three areas that are tactics, targets, and weapons. In tactics, there is Bombing, Armed assault, Assassination, Hijacking, Hostage taking and others. This shows a level of awareness on the part of the terrorist on how to execute their cause and how to hold their ground sending a clear message. Some of these tactics also have been perfected by certain groups. In the case of Targets, the selection also is quite meticulously done, be it the involvement of civilians or purely military personnel or facility.

It shows that terrorists do not just pick a target by accident but there seem to be a prior consideration that probably meets their required outcome and subsequent reactions. They seem to opt for more soft targets that put the authorities at loggerhead with the civilians. This is because most of these targets like transportation systems or commercial centres are hard to defend and secure without causing panic. In the case of weaponry, the statistics as shown largely stipulates that most attacks are achieved through explosives or armed assaults. Meaning there are greater use of guns and explosives in all manners.

Terrorist Group Dynamics

The dynamics of terrorist groups are a comprehensive issue, which needs deep concentration. When I read it through various sources, I found it as a topic of my interest. Being a counter terrorism researcher, I decided to highlight some dynamics of the terrorist group.

Normally, terrorist organisations strive to train young people from areas where the economic, political and social factor of the region are challenging and promote hate culture, anger, and feelings of hopelessness. This is ultimately true in the case of Afghanistan and Pakistan.

Through clear and shining glasses, we are looking at the issue to clarify the statistical patterns in the frequency and severity of violent attacks by terrorist organisations. Thus larger, more experienced organisations are deadlier because they attack more frequently, not because their attacks are deadlier, and large events are equally likely to come from large and small organisations. The attraction and identity of the terrorist group are thus moulded by the culture of life experienced outside of the terrorist group, which results in marginalization, alienation, and hate toward those perceived as responsible for their misery. However, terrorist groups do not stand still, they grow and respond to the challenging situation with their social, political resolve. In my understanding, the impact of group dynamics on terrorist decision making is deep. Provocative situational context is the first vehicle for terrorism, the impact of group dynamics has more implications than external factors. Religious motivations can also be tied to ethnic and nationalist identities, such as Kashmiri separatists combining their desire to break away from India.

A terrorist will evaluate what force protection measures are in effect in the vicinity of a target and determine a cost-benefit analysis. From these analyses and forms of study and surveillance, a terrorist will isolate the weaknesses of a target and exploit these weaknesses. The behaviour of terrorist groups may seem highly strategic and thus largely contingent; however, by taking a comparative approach in considering data on terrorist attacks, I find that surprising patterns emerge. In an interaction with a hostile external environment, the groupthink process intensifies as group cohesiveness and isolation becomes stronger. Having described the dynamics of the terrorist group, we next identify eleven basic tools that terrorist's use—with varying degrees of sophistication—to sustain these activities. The organisational tools are:

1. Training,

2. Publicity,

3. Operational space,

4. A guiding and motivating ideology,

5. Leadership,

6. Recruitment pools,

7. Ooperational security,

8. Command,

9. Control

10. Intelligence, and

11. Money.

For example, the organisation of the Taliban is based and located in Afghanistan and Pakistan. The main goal of the Taliban is the promulgation of Sharia Laws (Islamic law) and withdrawal of foreign forces from Afghanistan. They are fighting foreign and Afghan forces for years and receive weapons and funds from different sources, including the smuggling of narcotics and arms. Taliban is an extremist and a takfiri jihadist group, which justify the killing of those who are not associated with them.

Dr Gary LaFree has discussed the issue of terrorism, the 9/11 terrorist attacks, and the US operations against the Taliban in Afghanistan and Pakistan, and I am agreeing with him. In Taliban tactics, bombing, armed assault, assassination, hijacking, hostage-taking and others are mandatory. This shows a level of awareness on the part of the terrorist on how to execute their cause and how to translate their message into reality. After the fall of the Taliban regime in 2001, they associated with al Qaeda, reorganised and started attacking the US-allied countries, like Britain in 2005 and 2009, Spain, Mumbai, Bali, and several other countries. I have clarified the statistical patterns in the frequency and severity of violent attacks by the Taliban terrorist organisation. Thus larger, more experienced as the groups are deadly because it attacks more frequently.

Contrast between effectiveness and impact of terrorism

Terrorism as a tool to put a message through already shows its effectiveness, government and people give cognisance to the fact that an event has occurred and for such reason. For terrorists or groups and individuals with grievance using terrorism is an easier tool, cheap and loud. Terrorism at this time and age attracts more attention and sentiments though it might be just a minor incident. The publicity gotten from such events is a boost to groups, individuals and causes. It forces the hands of the state to react most of the time either in a positive or negative way. In the sense of effect, mostly temporary and wears off unless sustained over a longer period of time. So, a group has to constantly engage in their acts to affect a warranted result. For example, the constant attacks in Iraq made it hard for the government and the allied forces to govern but they modelled ways and means to incorporate the few Sunnis who wanted development.

Impact of terrorism is mostly permanent or the notion of a new paradigm shift because of terrorism. This has been increased use of technology all over the world to manage the movement of people. For example, deployment of biometric identifications, use of CCTVs, use of metal detectors and scanners. In some instances, laws have been changed to accommodate invasive searchers. There has been the formation of stringent financial laws to monitor the transfer of funds, especially in western countries. There has been increased profiling of individuals. Cross border travels have been more stringent with most countries instituting Visa requirement laws. More governments have increased their budgetary allocations to fight terrorism. Even enemy states are now cooperating for common goals, for example, U.S.A and Syria, U.S.A and Iran. Malls are now milling with police presence and security guards. In other countries, other crimes have spiked because of diverted attention, i.e. drug trafficking, robberies, burglaries.

Therefore, the effectiveness and impact of terrorism are totally different. One is short term while the other is permanent. The ideology of the Taliban is in operation in accordance with motivated ideology, recruitment and mobilisation components. Individual radicalisation is a specific process by which a man or women, old and young, or groups decide to adopt extreme religious or sectarian ideas.

Radicalisation by developing an extremist way of life and ideology, which justify violence is one possible pathway into terrorism involvement, but it is certainly not the only one. In the case of individual Radicalisation, it is important to know how individuals join an already Radicalised group.

A person can be Radicalised as a result of the perception of unjustified harm to him or loved ones. Most people who become the victims of Radicalisation do not understand about the individuals who made them victimised; their target of radical action. Terrorist groups often include people seeking revenge. Radicalism is like a live wire running through the state and society. It produces violence often when required as was obvious in Pakistan's case. Apart from Khyber-Pakhtunkhwa (KPK), which suffered repercussions of Taliban insurgency, the actual violence was fairly manageable. The terror attack on children school in Pakistan was a revenge attack of the Taliban groups or those are relative were killed by Pakistan army in the military operations in Waziristan and FATA regions.

Radicalisation can involve the movement of individuals and groups to legal and nonviolent political action or to illegal and violent political action. As we also found that Radicalisation refers to cases in which individuals or groups adopt a radical way of life or radical teaching of religion. Group grievance Radicalisation dynamics are similar to people who are primed by personal grievances. Sometimes, an uneven event forces an individual to react violently. According to the counter-terrorism analysis of Dr Matthew Francis, about the individual Radicalisation process: "It is perhaps the ideologies of groups which are the key area where a difference can be seen between radicalisation and violent radicalisation." Individual Radicalisation has its own culture. In Afghanistan and Pakistan, the culture of violence, terrorism and Radicalisation is quite different from the culture of Radicalisation, terrorism and violence of the West and Europe.

Global jihadism can be described as a conglomeration of extremism across the world. Global jihadism has specific motives but not linked to political Islam. Jihadists often criticise extremist groups. They believe that in doing so extremists have renounced Islamic law. They consider Western societies and brutal regimes as two sides of the same coin. From Afghanistan, Osama bin Laden started his jihadist campaign, while his teacher, Abdullah Azzam continued it until his death. Jihadist groups in the Muslim and non-Muslim world understand that violent struggle as necessary to eradicate obstacles for restoring Sharia.

In 1970, as evolution began operations in the Arab world. In Egypt, Akhwan al Muslimeen emerged with strong networks. Abdullah Azzam went to Afghanistan many times. After the Soviet withdrawal in 1989, many jihadists left Afghanistan. Mujahedeen arrived in Bosnia, Tajikistan and Chechnya to defend local Muslims against non-Muslim armies. In 1998, Kharijites movements emerged in South Asia and Europe. Some foreign fighters left Afghan-Pak to continue terrorist activities in other regions. There have been reports that many IJU and IMT militants have left Afghanistan for Syria where Seyfuddin Uzbek Jamaat, an IMT subsidiary, and Imam Bukhari Jamaat, an alleged subsidiary of the IJU, operate. At least several dozen militants have entered Syria via their channels and are now fighting there on the side of the armed opposition. In 1998, Zawahiri issued a FATWA against the United States and declared total war against it and its allies. On 11 September 2001, Al Qaeda attacked the United States, and later on, in 2002, attacked Bali, in 2003 Casablanca, in 2004 Madrid and in 2005 London. The United States invaded Iraq, which created Zarqawi. With the killing of Zarqawi, Global Jihad reached North and South Africa.

In Sudan, A radical Islamic group, Boko Haram, that kills innocent civilian trains its members in various African countries and receives military and financial support from Chad, Niger and Sudan. The group has close relations with Al Shabab and other Asian terrorist groups. Boko Haram bombed many Churches in the past two years. According to the Long War Journal recent report, just two months after targeting UN Office in Abuja, the sect launched a series of attacks in Northern Nigeria's military headquarter and in Maiduguri. The campaign of beheading non-Muslims in the name of religion including attacks on Churches and suicide bombing was condemned worldwide. In 2012, Human Rights Watch reported more 255 people were killed in various terror attacks. In Somalia, al-Shabab vowed to "connect the Horn of Africa jihad" to the one led by al-Qaeda in 2010.

In 2011, Bin Laden was killed in Pakistan. In 2013, ISI leader Abu Bakr al-Baghdadi announced the merger of his group and al-Qaeda's affiliate in Syria, al-Nusra Front, and the creation of Islamic State in Iraq and the Levant (ISIS or ISIL). The war in Iraq, Afghanistan, Syria, Yemen, Somalia and the re-emergence of violent extremist networks in South Ai, South East Asia and Africa badly affected the peaceful environment of Europe and the United Kingdom. The presence of strong financial networks of war criminals and sectarian mafia groups, their links with extremist groups in their countries of origin is a matter of great concern.

Case study: What is the Strategic Logic of the Taliban?

The suicide academies operating in South and North Waziristan region train suicide bombers from across the world. First, they train then brainwash and finally fix their prices. They export these human missiles to Afghanistan, Punjab, Chechnya, and Ingushetia, Russia and now they might export them to Europe, UK and the Arab world. Analysts believe that one of the reasons behind sabotaging schools is to keep children away from modern education. They have the agenda of destroying everything in Pakistan through all available means. They use children in their terrorist attacks, seduce young people and invite women to martyrdom mission. Once they are recruited and trained, they are threatening of dire consequences if they refuse to blow themselves up. In July 2009, Washington Times reported that Taliban are buying children as young as seven years old to use them as suicide bombers in attacks against the police and army targets. "The ongoing price for child bombers has been fixed $7,000 to $14,000; the price depends on how quickly the bomber is needed and how close the child is expected to get to the target." The newspaper reported.

In wars against terrorism, suicide bombers have become very effective tool than more powerful weapons, including rockets and missiles. Suicide bombing prospers because it has been seen to succeed. According to modern research on terrorism, terror groups are increasingly relying on suicide bombing to quickly achieve political goals. Now in Lebanon, Israel, Sri Lanka, India, Pakistan, Afghanistan, Yemen, Turkey, and Russia, suicide bombers have carried out suicide attacks against the government installations and the civilian population. Most suicide terrorism is undertaken as a strategic effort directed toward achieving particular political goals. The vast majority of suicide terrorist attacks are not isolated or random acts by individual fanatics but, rather, occur in clusters as part of a larger campaign by an organised group to achieve a specific political goal. Afghan Taliban has also set up several suicide training centres in north-eastern, Western and Southern parts of the country.

These training centres are now working on permanent bases. They receive money and other financial assistance from business community based outside Afghanistan. Long War Journal in one of its articles revealed that these terror centres have been established in eight districts of Kunar Province. Afghan and Pakistani teenagers who were kidnapped by Taliban men for recruiting reached Karachi and Peshawar carrying out target killings and a suicide attack.

A DIG police in Punjab revealed to me the fact that the main source of Taliban terror finance in Punjab is kidnapping which is now the single largest source of revenue. The ransoms paid tend to run high, ranging from $40,000 to $50,000.

In this debate, I would like to mention the perception of Mr Braniff as he discussed a range of terrorist group strategies and tactics, and I agree with him. In my selected group (Taliban), membership, resources, and organisational structure determine the capabilities of the group for carrying out terrorist operations in Afghanistan and Pakistan. Leadership is very important to keep unity intact. My selected organisation's leadership is united and traditionally strong. Normally, terrorist organisations strive to train young people from areas where the economic, political and social factor of the region are challenging and promote hate culture, anger, and feelings of hopelessness. The Taliban is doing the same and select people of the same background. This is ultimately true in the case of Afghanistan and Pakistan. The structure of Taliban determines its strengths and weaknesses. The Taliban group has established cells based on personal relationship, family or traditional relationships which are parallel to the organisational structure mentioned by Mr Braniff. These cells are used to control its members and carry out attacks against the government forces and civilians... However, with regard to the ideology, it maintains ideological unity among its members.

Taliban evaluates what force protection measures are in effect in the vicinity of a target. In the case of Targets, the selection also is quite meticulously done be it the involvement of civilians or purely military personnel or facility. It shows that the Taliban does not just pick a target by accident but there seem to be prior considerations that probably meet their required outcome and subsequent reactions. They seem to opt for more soft targets that put the authorities at loggerhead with the civilians. Taliban has four levels of commitment comprised of passive supporters, active supporters, cadre, and leaders. The group is using well organised system and network and respond to the attacks of US and NATO forces effectively.

The Taliban ideology which is based on a religious or single issue like the promulgation of Sharia (Islamic Law) lacks some specific political or nationalistic agenda. In chapter-3 of his "Military Guide to Terrorism in the Twenty-First Century" (15 August 2007), writer Lee Hamilton suggests: "The cell is the foundation building block of either organisation. Depending on how cells are linked to other elements, the structure will display one of three basic configurations: chain, hub and star, or all-channel networks".

Taliban has numerous motivations depending on their interests. The group has its own culture of terrorism, differing in ways of killing with the terrorist groups of South Asia. A recent study published by the international society of political psychology journal explored the above-mentioned dynamics by comparing the documents issued by terrorist groups to those issued by non-violent groups with the same belief system. Taliban carry out attacks against the Afghan National Army and civilians, the important thing here is that what is significant is how personal loyalties and strains and tensions, as well as loyalties to family and clan, are overlaid against national factor effects and international factor effects, that provide the backdrop to that series of interconnections, between stakeholders and dynamics to produce terrorist outcomes.

The most recent pattern of intense attacks by the Taliban in Afghanistan has put the credibility of the Afghan unity government and its security forces into question. Taliban has become a potential threat, benefiting from the changing loyalties of ethnic groups in the north and sectarian groups in the south and south-western parts of the country. The Ghani-Abdullah government is disunited on the national counter-terrorism strategy and stands at the crossroads. Both the chief executive and the president have different political priorities, which possibly caused their unsystematic approach to the ongoing, unbridled wave of terrorism. The massacre of 100 innocent civilians, including an Afghan national army soldier in the Ajristan district of Ghazni province, Afghanistan by IS forces, and the brutal killings of children in the army school in Peshawar have raised serious questions about the future of security and stability in South Asia. The Taliban claimed responsibility and called it a revenge attack for the Pakistan army's Operation Zarb-e-Azb in North Waziristan and FATA regions.

A Maryland University professor Mr Bill Braniff widely discussed the strategic logic and the provocation which is of much importance. "The Taliban, specifically, emphasize on provocation against the Afghan and Pakistani security forces and against the US and NATO presence in the country. They use different tactics. Its organisational ideology provides ground and is flexible enough to adapt to changing conditions, and its decision-making process allows for individual initiative.

After the US and NATO successful military operation in Afghanistan, and Pakistan, Taliban suffered a number of setbacks, but still is a successfully spawned a jihadist movement. The group continues to promote violence across South Asia and challenge nation-states. Basically, attrition is a very important idea because it gets out the importance of the constituency, especially in a democracy." In present-day Afghanistan and Pakistan, Taliban wants to continue fighting unless Islamic law is implemented in Afghanistan. The countless efforts made by a security official at the scene are laudable who strived hard to contain the militants at minimum harms and succeeded to some extent.

However, serious questions related to the plagued performance of security forces at entrances and deficient intelligence reports are raised at the poor performance that seemed short of timely coordination. How can explosive, automatic guns and suicide jackets laden car easily pass the security checkpoints across Afghanistan? Why there is no intelligence report prior to the incidence? The security institutions are liable for their negligence and poor performance. If the aforementioned drifts are not bridged then the future prospects of a perpetual deteriorated state of affairs can't be ruled out. A terrorist organisation can be structured in many different ways, depending on their objectives. Because, as we mentioned in the case of the Taliban, the structure can be in detriment modes in which it operates and performs. In my understanding, the structure of the Taliban has provided to its members limpid guidance for how to proceed. It is important that a clear structure definitely gives the Taliban a means to maintain order and resolve its organisational disagreements. The Taliban structure binds members together.

In general understanding, a well-organised structure of a group and organisation is the group strong skeleton, which defines the roles of members and it makes up a group's functioning and shows how everything fits together into a whole. The structure of the Taliban is well organised and strong; therefore, its organisation is a united entity in decision making. They follow one leader and receive an order from him. Taliban's internal factors such as target selection, operational pace, ideology, and stated goals shape its structure. In its recent definition and introduction of a terrorist group, Terrorism Research suggested that: "Terrorist groups that are associated with political activity or organisation will often require a more hierarchical structure, in order to coordinate terrorist violence with political action. It also can be necessary for a politically affiliated group to observe "cease-fires" or avoid particular targets in support of politicians on the issue of countering Taliban in the insurgency, Pakistan and Afghanistan need a well-established and coordinated countering strategy, and support of their citizens.

Case study: Al Qaeda in Afghanistan

Al Qaeda is the world most violent terrorist organisation, emerged in Afghanistan, and developed in a most threatening group in Iraq. For decades, terrorists have carried out attacks against non-combatant targets causing massive destruction by means of vicious assaults, but the recent violent attacks of al Qaeda in Afghanistan, Iraq and parts of Africa and the Middle East changed the perception of terrorism. Some say that al Qaeda emerged in the late 1980s when Arab mujahedeen came to Afghanistan for fighting to drive out occupying Soviet forces. Osama bin Laden was its leader and he, financially supported the groups. Since 1990s, al Qaeda emerged in the west and Europe with a new form. In general understanding, Al-Qaeda, a complex organisation, challenges Nations intelligence and national security apparatus for a quite long time. Al-Qaeda's organisational ideology provides common ground and is flexible enough to adapt to changing conditions, and its decision-making process allows for individual initiative. After the US and NATO successful military operation in Afghanistan, Pakistan and the Arab world, Al-Qaeda suffered a number of setbacks, but still is a successfully spawned an expansionist global jihadist movement.

The group continues to promote violence across the world and challenge nation-states in South Asia, Middle East and the Arab world. Interestingly, majority people in the West became aware of al-Qaeda after the attacks of September 11, 2001, while al Qaeda can be traced back to the 1996 bombings of the Khobar Towers in Saudi Arabia, the 1998 attacks on US Embassies in

Kenya and Tanzania, and the 2000 assault on the USS Cole in Yemen. This terrorist organisation works in a much opaquer information environment than the truth movement does. When a statement or action is attributed to al-Qaeda, it is almost impossible to verify who is really behind it. Now, al Qaeda has become a bigger challenge in case of al Shabab, Boko Haram, Taliban and IS in Afghanistan, Pakistan, Middle East and Africa. How to effectively counter violent extremism is a dilemma that bedevils leaders and policymakers the world over. In this country, as elsewhere, we have seen that military force alone is insufficient to uproot militancy; the battle to counter terrorism must be a multifaceted one. Participants from over 60 countries, as well as the UN, EU and OIC, reached a similar conclusion at a summit to counter violent extremism, organised by the White House, which ended in Washington. .

US War on Terror Policy in the region

The point was driven home by none other than Barack Obama. It is indeed welcome that world leaders are adopting a nuanced view of global militancy and taking pains not to link terrorism with "any religion, nationality [or] civilisation". Yet, perhaps there needs to be a greater realisation and acknowledgement in Western capitals, especially Washington, that force, particularly interventions directed at 'unfriendly' regimes, as well as the use of extremist proxies, has played a major role in fuelling modern global militancy.

For example, removing strongmen in Iraq and Libya through force has resulted in the meltdown of the state, paving the way for extremists to create space for themselves.

The use of militant proxies has also not been abandoned; while the mujahedeen were supported by the West together with Pakistan and Saudi Arabia to block the Soviets' onward march during the Afghan jihad, the use of fundamentalist fighters in Syria to topple Bashar al-Assad's regime remains an instrument of policy.

Hence when critics say the rise of the self-styled Islamic State owes much to the West plan to remove Assad through Syrian 'rebels', there is indeed an element of truth in this. Where the use of extremist proxies is concerned, Pakistan itself has experienced the painful blowback of such policies. Muslim governments share equal responsibility for creating the conditions that breed extremism. Many Muslim states are either absolute monarchies or sham democracies, which disallow their people political and social rights. Hence when forces — including violent Islamists — challenge autocratic rulers, they find support within the populace. Also, when Western states support Muslim dictators who crush internal dissent, Muslim populations' mistrust of the West grows. For efforts against militancy to succeed, some principles must be acknowledged: that democracy cannot be imposed through regime change; that extremist proxy must not be used against geopolitical rivals; and that autocrats in Muslim states must not be aided in their efforts to counter popular calls for democracy.

The IS arrival in Khorasan

The arrival of thousands of IS soldiers, commanders and their families in Afghanistan is a cause for alarm. The Afghan news agency Pajhwok reported the killing of a Taliban commander by IS forces in Logar province. However, Mohammad Omar Safi, the governor of Kunduz province, warned that IS had established its networks across the province. IS declared the creation of the Khorasan Shura, a leadership council for Afghanistan and Pakistan, composed almost entirely of former Tehreek-e-Taliban Pakistan (TTP) leaders. The Taliban and IS have equally established their military wings along the borders of Turkmenistan, Uzbekistan, Tajikistan and China's Xinjiang province. The IS forces are trying to enter the Muslim majority provinces of China while China is talking with the Taliban, which has already announced allegiance to Abu Baker al-Baghdadi. In 2014, an Azerbaijan newspaper reported that IS's minister of state security, Abdul Waheed

Khudair Ahmed, had stated that IS would reach Azerbaijan in the near future. His argument rested on the fact that the Caucasian jihadist fighters in IS would be seeking to avenge the blood of their martyrs who had fallen in Syria. These and other terrorist organisations that operate across the country have further wrapped the blanket smothering the Afghan state.

People across the country continue to join the IS networks. In Kunduz province, an IS commander maintains an army of 400 fighters. Moreover, across the Durand Line, IS commanders have formed an alliance with Taliban groups to deploy them under a unified military command of the TTP, the Khyber based Lashkar-e-Islam, Jamaat-ul-Ahrar and IS Khorasan chapter. In the presence of these challenges and developments, the state has embroiled itself in a deep crisis and is regressing back to conditions prior to the civil war in the 1990s in which Kabul was destroyed. The recent political and military rapprochement between Afghanistan and Pakistan is being perceived as an incomplete and reluctant love story by diplomatic circles in Kabul. The Pakistan army has its own foreign policy, its own counterterrorism strategy, and its own way of conflict resolution, and does not share several of its diplomatic and military deals with the democratic government of the country.

In Afghanistan, the unity government also does not share its hidden agenda and international engagements with parliament and politicians. This is perceived by experts to be akin to a secret diplomacy. In Pakistan, the army is building its own image while the role it plays in Afghan reconciliation cannot be identified in a few words. Key national policies are being dictated by the khakis, not by the elected government. The army determines Pakistan's national security threats, the Afghan and Kashmir policies, and challenges and decides how to deal with them. The recent interview of the former President, General Musharraf, with a UK newspaper (Guardian) once again caused misunderstanding and distrust between the two states. Mr Musharraf admitted that when he was in power, the ISI had sought to undermine the government of Hamid Karzai because Karzai had "helped India stab Pakistan in the back". "In President Karzai's times, yes, indeed, he was damaging Pakistan and therefore we were working against his interest. Obviously, we had to protect our own interest," Musharraf said.

However, he shamelessly admitted that his government had been responsible for the killings of innocent Afghan men, women and children in the Inter-Services Intelligence's (ISI's) constituted suicide attacks. General Musharraf said that the ISI trained the Taliban after 2001 to undermine the Karzai government dominated by India's supported non-Pashtuns. "Obviously we were looking for some groups to counter this Indian action against Pakistan," he said.

This interview deeply disappointed Afghan politicians and members of civil society, who started asking whether Pakistan was playing a new game with their country.

Though the Afghan president has categorically said that peace without Pakistan is impossible, Afghan parliamentarians and intellectual circles ask why the democratic government in Pakistan does not react to the efforts of the army and ISI, and why the army is doing the job of the civilian government. The silence of the Pakistani president, parliamentarians, politicians and the prime minister on the diplomatic role of the armed forces and ISI in Afghanistan has raised serious questions about the military and civilian divide. Finally, in case of such resentment and loath between Afghanistan and Pakistan, countering Taliban can be a difficult task. They need a cohesive and well-organized strategy. The recent talks between Taliban, Afghan and Pakistani governments can address the demands of the Taliban, and I hope they will change their strategy. If the distrust between the two states remains the same, the Taliban can create many challenges for the security and law enforcement agencies of Afghanistan and Pakistan.

Types of Terrorism and Ideologies of Terrorists

There are many kinds of Terrorists and many types of terrorism operating around the globe. Few are famous for 100 years, few are for a half century and few are newly formed. In my point of persuasion based on my study and research, there are 4 types of terrorism active in the world.

1. Offensive Terrorism
2. Defensive terrorism
3. Resistive Terrorism
4. Supportive Terrorism

Above types of terrorism has different ideology and psychological impacts. Some terrorist's ideology is to create fear and tension in the public, some keep the focus on to demolish military infrastructure and some do the terrorist activity to paralyze the Government and some are to demolish the economic system. To understand which type of terrorism is actively operated in which region is not easy to judge or analysis, it needs close eyes or research on the regions and their movements. Some organisations were and are supported and funded by the Governments and some are by the public and some are surviving through crimes. Every organisation has their own motives and separate agenda, some organisations have a religious background, some have the secular background and some have nationalism.

Marxism background. Those organisations who were created or born in the midst of Middles east most were nationalists and Marxist ideology. Those organisations supported/ funded by Jordan, Egypt, Syria or Qatar were purely nationalists.

The question is what is the difference between three most famous Terrorist organisations: 1-IRA (Irish Republic Army) 2-Hamas 3-Taliban.

> ➤ IRA: The IRA was/is a Nationalist cum religious Organisation.

> ➤ HAMAS: Hamas is a Religious cum Nationalist Organisation.

> ➤ TALIBAN: Taliban is a Religious cum Political Organisation.

One most common thing in all above organisation is their political role within the state. They all terrorist organisations have or had somehow a political contribution in the political system. They had two types of agendas, one is within the border and the other is the cross border. Political and social type of agenda they use within the state and terrorism agenda they use the cross border to gain their international political benefits.

Now the thing is this; these are they all three organisations come in 1st type of Terrorism category mentioned above or 2nd, 3rd and 4th? Some counterterrorism experts think they all come in the 3rd category of terrorism, which is resistance terrorism and they often call resistance movements. Their all terrorism actions were/are against the occupying forces or Governments. IRA's terrorism activities are against the UK Government on Northern Ireland and IRA believe UK Government occupied their territory, Hamas's activities are against the Israel Government only for the same reasons and Taliban's actions are against the Western forces in Afghanistan with the same reasons. I personally think that these all three terrorist organisations come in all types of terrorism, but it totally depends on their activities and depends the occupier forces' actions against them to put them in different categories in different circumstances. These organisations are resistance movement which turned to offensive and sometimes defensive positions and start their terrorist activities in the offensive and defensive terminology and all are supported by some Governments who always promoted terrorism to gain their political benefits.

The IRA was a terrorist group only once it was formed, but now it is a strong movement which lives within the Irish people and in the same way Hamas was the only group once created, but now it became movement and living within the Palestinians and Taliban was only a group supported by Pakistan and now entire Afghan population to support them against the western forces and corrupt Government backed by the west.

There are two types of Taliban organisations. One group is fighting on Afghan land against western forces and others are fighting on Pak land against Pak forces. Both use the same techniques in resistance which call Suicide Bombing but their objects are different from each other. One believes Sharia law to be implemented on Pak land and second want western forces out of Afghan soul.

Hamas established in 1982 when people of Palestinians were defeated on every step of resistance, when Arab governments lost all their wars and against Israel and lost their territories. Hamas was formed on the religious pattern because all other resistance movements were created on the slogan of nationalism, not on the name of Islam so all failed, but now people kept hope into Hamas as an Islamic resistance movement. Most Palestinians were/are nationalist and seculars not very religious that's why Hamas changed its formation and it became Nationalist cum religious resistance organisation. Hamas is far different from the Taliban by their ideology, their strength and through their support. Their Ideologies came from or influenced by Ikhwans (Muslims Brotherhood) and Ikhwanul Muslimoon was created in 1926 during the First World War.

Ikhwan opened their branches in many countries including Iraq, Yemen, Jordan, Syria, Egypt and Palestine. After the creation of Israel, their one branch splits into two. One formed in West Bank who was controlled by Jordanian Ikhwans and second formed in the Gaza strip which was controlled by Egyptian Ikhwan. After around 30 years Ikhwan based in Gaza strip created new

Military organisation which called HAMAS. Hamas was/is the branch of Ikhwanul Muslimoon (Muslim Brotherhood). Hamas is influenced by Ikhwans and their ideology followed the Ihsanul Bala and Syadina Qutub of Ikhwanul Muslimoon. Saudi Arabia was/is always against the Ikhwan because Ikhwans fully supported the group called Kuhaymans who once attacked on the Holy Ka'bah (House of God) in Makkah. This is why Saudi backed general SISI of Egypt to overthrow the Government of Morsi (Ikhwan) and Saudi always stands against Hamas because of their roots of Ikhwans. Everyone knows Iran is a great enemy of Saudi Arabia and Iran always supported, funded, armed and trained Hamas militants because it knows Hamas is against Saudi Arabia and Saudi Arabia is against the Hamas.

When Morsi Government collapsed by the Army in Egypt there was only one country who strongly not only condemned but oppose the policy of Saudi Arabia in Egypt which is Qatar. Qatar Government is always backed Ikhwans by hook or crook that's why all big leadership of Hamas is under the shelter of Qatar and Qatar rejected all steps taken by the Egypt army against the Ikhwans and because of the opposed against the policy of Saudi Arabia, Saudi and Qatari relations are intense at the moment. Taliban Ideology is the same ideology of Ikhwans that's why the Taliban fully supported Al Qaida (AQ) because AQ was influenced by Ikhwan/Qutubi ideologically. If we see Ikhwan ideology is behind every famous Islamic terrorist organisation and it grows day by day and it is the key responsibilities of Muslim countries/rules to educate their people against this great threat of Ikhwan's Ideology.

Case Study: LeT (Lashkar -e- Toaba- Pakistan)

LeT is a Pakistan based globally recognised terrorist organisation, fully operates within and cross borders of Pakistan LeT fighters used automatic rifles, pistols and explosive devices against the Indian army and civilians. 90% attacked carry out by LeT terrorist were used by common weapons which are commonly available everywhere. LeT is the militant group of JuD and JuD is the religious Salafist and non-political organisation which strongly rooted in Pakistani population. The ideology of LeT is based on Islamist extremism, which uses Quranic verses and hadith and manipulates the exact message and induces into the person's mind. The Islamist extreme message then generates hatred emotions and make people ready to do anything harsh towards the opposing religion/nation/country in revenge. LeT always uses religious extremism to recruit more people from every corner of the country to fight for the cause of Islam to dominate on Hindus. Islamic Extremism is totally based on the Ideology, without an ideology, no one can take any extreme action in a world. My field of interest is how an ideology could be generated? I personally keep focus on the mind process that generates an ideology, but how a mind-process works! There are many stages to run the process in the mind. There are some good and some bad stages of the mind process that directly effect on a person's behaviour and personality. The question is this how these stages work? The stages work through the messages which call "unwanted messages".

These unwanted messages grow the negative stages that run the negative process of the Mind, and the mind generates the extreme ideology and an ideology generates the extremism and the extremism creates extremists. LeT's basic rule to recruit more people is religious wise emotionally blackmailing. They create baseless stories and show the picture how Hindus rape Muslim women and humiliated

pictures of young Muslim men and how the Indian Army torture them because they are Muslims. They create heat and anger in their minds to promote religious extremism in their behaviour and use them for their religious agenda against their opposite religion. Most terrorists use violence to spread their ideology/belief to others by force and to advance an ideological goal. This claim fully covers the ideology of specific group LeT because it has already used violence in their operational targeted areas to promote their ideology to achieve the religious and political goals. LeT uses the religious emotions as a grievance to recruit youngsters and use the religious idea "Every Muslim should military trained to defend the Islam" and induce their ideology into their minds to create radical emotion. LeT uses this grievance, ideology and mobilization gather more people to their radical cause and Dr Bill already explained these three main elements that organisation uses in their radicalisation model.

LeT is a militant branch of an organisation which is fully rooted with the Pakistani people through their charity work. This is called a hybrid terrorist organisation that on one hand, they use terror acts and on the other hand to use charity work to gain trust, sympathy, funds and recruit more people within the population. JuD is using the same structure which Hamas uses in Gaza. LeT's organisational structure is based on three things, 1- leadership 2-charity work 3- networking. Fewer people know that Hafiz Saeed was not a founder of JuD but a renounce Salafi scholar, well populated for his religious doctrine in South Asia and in Saudi Arabia "BadiUdin Shah Rashidi" who with the help of Mehmood Bahazauq (a Juhyman Militant leader who attacked at the Grand Mosque of Makkah in 1979). Hafiz Saeed was replaced since Rashidi's death. So, the one reason of organisational structure was the leadership of the Salafi scholars and second is the charitable work.

Goals: The goals of the chosen organisation are to promote religious extremism in the region and use violence to create fear to opposite. LeT aims not only to eject India from Kashmir, but also seeks to re-establish Islamic rule over the entire Indian Union.

According to the report published by SSI (Strategic Studies Institute) "LeT's goal is to establish an independent homeland for Muslims in southern and northern India. Nonetheless, the LeT has forged relationships with militant movements (though the strength of these the source of much debate) in Afghanistan,

Bosnia, the Palestinian territories, and Kashmir in order to pool resources, share experience, and to improve the effectiveness of their operations.

Pakistani intelligence agency ISI is behind the LeT to achieve the political benefit to use the hot issue of Kashmir against India. Hafiz Saeed is playing a key role for the ISI to de-stabilise India and create more independent states within the state. Speaking to journalists Hafiz Saeed mentioned LeT's hidden agenda against India, He stated "The jihad in Kashmir would soon spread to entire India. Our Mujahedeen would create three Pakistanis India." LeT is organised in a militaristic fashion with a chief commander, provisional commander, district commander, battalion commander, and so on. The group also has a policy-making body that comprises an Amir (chief), Naib Amir (deputy chief), and various other strategists that are organized in a hierarchal fashion. Provocation: LeT always uses this strategy to provoke the Indian government to take action against the people of Kashmiris and LeT then use victimisation technique to recruit more people to rise against their democratic government. LeT is one of the most dangerous groups operating in Kashmir and throughout India. One of their provocation strategies was to torch the old religious shrine in Srinagar which calls "SHIRE OF BILL" and blamed to Indian army and gained great sympathy from the people of Kashmir.

Tactics (Weapons)

LeT uses very simple and common weapons, there are few reasons of using common weapons 1- These weapons are easy to carry and cross the Pak border to enter into Indian Kashmir 2- These weapons are simple, automatic and easy to train and use. 3- These weapons are widely available in Pakistan and Kashmir with low cost. LeT use, especially the common weapon like AK47, Pistols and small type of bombs like hand grenades and light weight Rocket launchers which easily carry on the back. Most times LeT uses the Gruella technique "Hit and run" and in this tactic, they use light weight arms which are mentioned above. Fight till death is the type of suicide attack. LeT often uses this suicide tactic which they call "Fedayeen" and this tactic LeT used in the Parliament attack in Delhi and Mumbai attack and its militants fought till death.

To counter the LeT strategy, it needs to generate awareness within people that they make differentiate the Takfiri Jihad, Extreme Religious Jihad and the Real Jihad (Self-purification). To stop their public speeches, impose a ban on their media network, to strict scrutiny at their schools, limited their movements, keep an eye on their religious speeches. The most worrying thing about this Organisation is that their sleeping cell is available across Europe to include Britain and the US and Canada.

According to Pakistani officials, a large portion of the funds sent from Britain was siphoned off and used to prepare the attacks; and out of the US$10million that was originally sent, much of which was likely sent to Jamaat-ud-Dawa, less than half was used in relief operations.

Unfortunately, LeT is fully supported by the state, it is a state-sponsored International terrorist organisation that carry on the fight not only in Kashmir but inside India, but in Afghanistan, Bosnia, Chechnya, Philippine, Kosovo, Syria and Iraq and I fear LeT will reach in Gaza and fight against the state of Israel along with Hamas. LeT leaders always respectfully released from the Pakistani prisons by the court orders.

Case Study: Boko Haram

The yester years established Takfiri Jihadist groups in Pakistan and Afghanistan, with the financial assistance of the Arab world now turned their arms on their Arab friends. They trained their Arab and African friends for fighting government forces, carrying out suicide attacks and making bombs. From Al Shabab to Boko Haram and Houthies, members of all militant groups of the Arab and African region are now professional fighters. In Nigerian violence, though ethnic factor is dominant, religious sectarianism emerged as the most potentially explosive social division. Violence introduced several social changes to the fragmented society and widened distances between Muslim and Christians in 1980. In 1980, for the first time, the Maitatsine sect started attacking opponents which resulted in eleven days emergency in Kano, Nigeria. The Kano riots were suppressed by the army in which 4,000 people killed. In 1981, when Ameer of Kano was deposed, extremist sects started attacking government installations and public properties. In 1982, followers of Maitatsine sect attacked opponents in which 188 civilians and 18 police killed. In 1984, members of the proscribed sect attacked Yola. In 1985 and again in 1988, more innocent people were killed and thousands of houses were set to fire.

Socioeconomic conditions that supported the existence of Maitetsine violence in 1980 were relevant to the Boko Haram uprising. Mass poverty, inequality in education sectors, illiteracy, unemployment and corruption in government institutions cause an unending civil war in Nigeria. Moreover, social breakdown according to the Times report made the country so prone to violent sectarianism.

Abimbola Adesoji in his recent research article has analysed the crisis in Nigeria and understands that Maitatsine's attacks caused many crises in the country: "The Maitatsine uprising in 1980 in

Kano, 1982 in Kaduna and Bulumkutu in 1984 in Yola and 1985 in Bauchi, obviously the first attempt at imposing a religious ideology on secular, independent Nigeria, marked the beginning of ferocious conflict and crisis in Nigeria." Sectarian war between Muslim and Christian sects in Nigeria started in 1987 on schools and university levels while from 1990 to 2000, attacks on each other religious places stopped. In 2002, with the establishment of Boko Haram sect, sectarian violence again started dancing in the streets of Nigeria. N.D Danjibo, in his research paper, has discussed the troubled journey of the sect in detail. In page six, he has introduced the leader of Boko Haram, Mr. Yusuf in these words:

"The leader of the Boko Haram Movement, Yusuf, was a secondary school drop-out who went to Chad and Niger Republic to study the Quran. While in the two countries, he developed radical views that were abhorrent to Westernisation and modernisation. Like the late Maitatsine, Yusuf got back to Nigeria and settled in Maiduguri and established a sectarian group in 2001 known as the Yusufiyya, named after him. The sect was able to attract more than 280,000 members across Northern Nigeria as well as in Chad and Niger Republic. Yusuf began his radical and provocative preaching against other Islamic scholars such as Jafar Adam, Abba Aji and Yahya Jingir and against established political institutions.

From 2010 to 2012, thousands of innocent civilians were killed by sectarian armies of different sects while members of Boko Haram started the killings of Christians in various places. Boko Haram is an anti-Western and anti-Christian Muslim religious sect. In Hausa language, Boko Haram is translated as Western education is Haram or sinful. In July 2009, Boko Haram killed more than 1000 people. This Islamic fundamentalist group is basically called Jamaatul Ahlussunna. The sect was formed by Muhammad Yusuf in the city of Maiduguri in 2002 and converted into a takfiri Jihadist group in 2009. According to their religious philosophy, they abhor western education and working in civil service. The sect propagates the interaction with the Western world is Haram and opposes Christians. Boko Haram is trying to impose Sharia law in Northern Nigeria. After the killing of Muhammad Yusuf, Boko Haram carried out its first terror attack in Bomo in 2010 which resulted in the killing of four civilians. In 2012 Abu-Bakr Shekau took control of the group and under his leadership, the group's terror cell killed more than 900 innocent people. Boko

Haram is considered a terrorist sect in Nigeria and, according to the CIA; the group is believed to be associated with al Qaeda.

A radical Islamist group, Boko Haram, that kills innocent civilian trains it members in various African countries and receives military and financial support from Chad, Niger and Sudan. The group has close relations with Al Shabab and other Asian terrorist groups. Boko Haram bombed many Churches in the past two years. According to the Long War Journal recent report, just two months after targeting UN Office in Abuja, the sect launched a series of attacks in Northern Nigeria's military headquarter and in Maiduguri. The campaign of beheading non-Muslims in the name of religion including attacks on Churches and suicide bombing was condemned worldwide. In 2012, Human Rights Watch reported more 255 people were killed in various terror attacks.

Terror network of Boko Haram in the United Kingdom is strongly active with its violent and hate campaign and can cause security problems during the Olympic Games in London because it receives substantial financial support from various groups and individuals within the country. The group has established a strong network here while more than 200,000 Nigerians are living in the UK and some of them support Boko Haram in many ways. The Christian Broadcasting Network recently reported that Iran and Libya are the source of arms smuggling to Boko Haram. According to the Nigerian Tribune (13 February 2012) report, the UK based group al Muntada Trust and charities in Saudi Arabia provide financial assistance to Boko Haram. News reports confirmed that one of the largest Somali groups in the UK lives close to the Olympic site while al Shabab terrorist group has strong roots in the United Kingdom. Police in Britain strictly watches the movements of suspected people to prevent the influx of terrorists into London. British members of Boko Haram, Taliban, Pakistani extremist groups and al Shabab are participating in civil wars in Somalia, Afghanistan, Pakistan and Nigeria.

Chief of Britain most competent Security Service has already warned that there is a significant number of UK residents training with al Shabab. Adesoji Abimbola also explored the terror link of Boko Haram and its training facilities in various Muslim states in his report: "The loud speculation in the Nigerian and foreign press about the activities of such groups as the Takfiri Group for Preaching and Combat in Algeria, Tablighi Jamaat from Pakistan and Wahhabi missionaries from Saudi Arabia in Northern Nigeria, as well as the reported training of some fundamentalists in al Qaeda camps in some foreign countries, offer proof of Boko Haram's links with fundamentalist groups around the world, however tenuous." Author and political analyst, N.D Danjibo, in his recent research report on Nigerian sectarian violence have described the role of religion in Nigeria influential which manifests itself as a potent force in the politico-religious development in the country.

On the issue of sectarian violence in Nigeria, Mr. N.D Danjibo understands: "there is a lot more than ideological Radicalisation to be taken into account to understand the reasons for sectarian violence in Nigeria. Religion will continue to be a reckoning force in Nigeria, but more potent will be the sectarian movements that will ever be ready to continue to engage the Nigerian state." According to intellectual circles in Nigeria, the perceived failure of the government to prevent the terror acts of BH is likely to lead to an increased in vigilant attacks by civilians. Finally, it must be born in mind that majority of Nigerian Muslim reject the anti-Western stance of Boko Haram and say greater interaction with the west is more important.

Hate Crime vs Terrorism

Now a day there are many debates, arguments and emotionally comments on the media, especially on social media that "if a Muslim kill someone it is to consider as a terrorist act and if non-Muslim kills any Muslim it is to consider as a hate crime". These types of arguments and balms started after the killing of three Muslims in California, USA when a white man killed three Muslims and it was considered a hate crime and Islamophobia. I would like to highlight some facts and figure that would help those who have no knowledge what is the difference between an act of terrorism and the act of hate crime. No doubts there are many similarities between the act of terror and the act of a hate crime, but there are many ways behind that make separate both actions.

A hate crime can be committed with a very narrow perspective of the impact that could have on people. For example, one person or a group of people could kill someone based on his/her skin colour without thinking of the media attention that the act would garner. It could be unplanned. Terrorist acts necessarily rely on media attention to bring attention to the terrorist organisation's cause, and to frighten the public. Terrorist activities are intended to make victims of people that have not actually been injured. Certain hate crimes are definitely a form of terrorism, and terrorism is also done out of hate, but they are not actually one and the same. A hate crime is a kind of terrorist act that's why it has a special status. It is meant to cause fear not just in the victim, but all those in the same category as the victim. A lot of terrorist acts are designed to go after a broad group of people, but it can be narrow. The goal of both is to create terror in a group of people.

According to Dilks "while there are a lot of similarities between hate crimes and acts of terrorism, the distinction comes in that acts of terror are planning attacks that are done to draw attention to some cause, rather than to inflict harm or suffering on a particular identity group".

Here are the main differences between a hate crime and an act of terrorism, according to Hodge and Dilks:

Hate crime:

> ➢ Additional charge that adds severity of punishment

> ➢ Used to send a message to perpetrators, victims and other community members who share the identity.

> ➢ Often spontaneous and fuelled by drugs/alcohol.

Terrorism:

> ➢ Orchestrated and often part of a series of events.

> ➢ Often associated with formal organisation or group.

> ➢ May mobilize an entire response force (Police, intelligence agencies & Army).

There are many acts committed by Muslims around the world that considered hate crimes rather than acts of terrorism, I mention here one case that was happening on 4th July 2002 when an Egyptian immigrant shot two people at the Israeli Airlines counter at the Los Angeles International Airport who are traveling to Israel and was shot dead by a security guard. The crime was recorded as a hate crime not a terrorist. The FBI had so far refused to call the shooting a terrorist act because it did not know the Egyptian man to be affiliated with any terrorist groups. The bureau is investigating the attack as a possible hate crime, or as the desperate act of a depressed man. The American press, for the most part, has accepted the FBI's shrugged-shoulders classification. There are many acts committed against the Jews in Europe, but that act was not considered as terrorism, but a hate crime which calls Anti-Semitic. Jews never mourned that why these acts considered as hate crime rather than terrorism, but they know the fact and intention behind the attacks.

Both are crimes of intent. When a federal hate-crime bill was up for passage in 1998, Sen.

Ted Kennedy (D-Mass.) even made the case that "hate crimes are a form of terrorism." By the FBI's numbers, hate crimes have directly affected the lives of more Americans than terrorism, though in the past couple of years' terrorism has left far deader; of the nearly 10,000 hate crimes committed in the year 2000, only 19 were murders. Racism is the main tool towards hate crime because racial hatred causes someone to commit a crime against the person whom he hated because of his colour, culture, race or religion and language. These acts come under the hate crime act individually.

According to the report published in the Guardian newspaper in 2006 and it showed that "Nearly half of all victims of racially motivated murders in the last decade have been white, according to official figures released by the Home Office". The data, released under Freedom of Information legislation, shows that between 1995 and 2004 there have been 58 murders where the police consider a racial element played a key part. Out of these, 24 have been where the murder victim was white.

In March 2004 a white Scottish teenager, Kriss Donald, was bundled into a car while walking in the Pollokshields area of Glasgow. He was later beaten, stabbed 13 times, and set on fire. British Pakistani Daanish Zahid was found guilty by unanimous verdict of the charges of racially aggravated murder.

In the same year Christopher Yates, 30, a white man, was beaten to death in an assault by a group of drunken Asian youths as he walked home in Barking, east London. Peter Fahy, the Chief Constable of Cheshire said 24 white victims also included those who were Jewish, 'dark-skinned' Europeans or gypsies. In addition, seven of those were killed by white attackers, four by black, six by Asian, with seven whose racial background was not identified. Overall, there have been 10 black victims and 16 Asian victims. Of the 58 race murders, 18 have been where a white attacker has killed a black or Asian individual and another 14 where one member of a minority group has murdered another for racial reasons.

According to the NCB report published in April 2014 "There are 939 active hate groups in the United States - a 56 percent increase since 2000, according to the Southern Poverty Law Centre. The number of such groups surged in response to President Barack Obama's election and the economic downturn - growing from 888 in 2008 to 1,007 in 2012 - before falling back slightly last year, according to Mark Potok, who tracks extremist groups for the SPLC. Members of these groups and others were involved in 5,796 "incidents" in 2012, the most recent year for which the FBI has compiled data. While that number declined from the 6,222 incidents reported in the prior year, 7,164 people were victimized".

As defined by the Hate Crime Statistics Act of 1990, hate crimes are "crimes that manifest evidence of prejudice based on race, gender or gender identity, religion, disability, sexual orientation, or ethnicity." For reporting purposes, it does not matter whether or not the perpetrators of the crime were ever charged with a hate crime.

According to the FBI Uniform Hate crime report from 1995 to 2012:

> Race/ ethnicity/origins – 88,736 victims

> Religion- 24,872 victim

> Sexual orientation- 21,788 victims

> Disability- 835 victims

> Multiple- Bias- 90 victims

Hate crimes exist in every country, every society and in every culture, which are dealt with as a hate crime by police services, not as terrorism. According to the report written by Kathleen Deloughery of University at Albany, State University of New York, USA that "Prior research has frequently drawn parallels between the study of hate crimes and the study of terrorism.

Yet, key differences between the two behaviours may be under appreciated in extant work. Terrorism is often an "upward crime," involving a perpetrator of lower social standing than the targeted group. By contrast, hate crimes are disproportionately "downward crimes," usually entailing perpetrators belonging to the majority or powerful group in society and minority group victims. The latter difference implies that hate crimes and terrorism are more akin to distant relatives than close cousins".

The primary difference between these types of crime is the motive behind the act. While there are no single, comprehensive definitions of hate crimes and terrorism, the Federal Bureau of Investigation (FBI) uses these working definitions: Hate crime (also known as bias crime) is a criminal offense committed against a person, property, or society that is motivated, in whole or in part, by the offender's bias against a race, religion, ethnic/national-origin group, or sexual-orientation group.

Terrorism is the unlawful use of force or violence against persons or property to intimidate or coerce a government, the civilian population, or any segment thereof, committed to further political or social objectives.

According to the justice committee for hate crimes in the US defined the hate crimes as a crime committed by hate groups or offenders and those committed by terrorist groups are often very similar, both in method and in effect. For example, a person acting from a motive of religious bias might use an incendiary device (one that causes a fire, such as a Molotov cocktail) to burn down a mosque, church, or synagogue.

A terrorist group might use the same type of device to burn down a government building. In both cases, the results are property damage, intimidation, and possibly even the deaths of or injuries to innocent people. One thing I mention here that we must not forget the psychological impacts behind the hate crime because it is exactly like other crime and terrorist act, but especially hate crimes are different from other crimes in that the offender, whether purposefully or not- is sending a message to members of a given group that they are unwelcome and unsafe in a particular neighbourhood, community, school, workplace or another environment. Hate crimes are often intended to threaten entire communities and do so. According to the American Psychological Association "Hate crimes are any felony or violent crime based on prejudice against a particular group. They are prejudice's most extreme expression. Compared to other crimes, hate crimes have a broader impact on victims and communities because they target core aspects of identity".

What sets hate crimes apart from other acts of violence is the psychological damage that they leave behind. Although any type of victimization carries with its psychological consequences, certain types of emotional reactions are more frequent among survivors of hate crimes. These feelings include depression, anxiety, fear, stress and anger. Before considering any act emotionally, we must consider internal and outer impacts of the act and must see the intention of the actor who committed the act rather than it is an act of terrorist or an act of hate crime. The definitions of both crimes to make separate accordingly and Law system deals both crimes, according to the definition of the lawmakers.

Chapter 3

Suicide Terrorism, Rational or Irrational

A suicide attack is an operational method in which the perpetrator knows it costs his or her life. This characteristic distinguishes the suicide attack from any other acts of terrorism. It places this action in the psychological realm and requires the suicide bomber to create a sort of tunnel vision. A cognitive solution for the gruesome action to come. The suicide bombers and indeed the terrorists' organisational goal is to spread fear and panic within society, instil fear and the feeling of helplessness regarding the inability to prevent such attack. Operationally, suicide attacks require no escape plan and reduce the fear of the perpetrator being caught and interrogated afterwards.

The number of suicide attacks has skyrocketed over the last two decades. Appearing first as a threat in Lebanon in the 1980s (in 1981: Al Dawa against the Iraqi Embassy and in 1983: The Hezbollah-led campaign of suicide attacks against Western targets) and then in Sri Lanka (1987: The Liberation Tigers of Tamil Eelam (LTTE) against a Sri Lanka Army camp). The phenomenon of suicide attacks has spread exponentially since then. Affected countries include, among others: Israel (1994), Turkey (1995) India (1999), Pakistan (1999), Russia (2000), the United States (2001), Kenya (2002), Saudi Arabia (2003), Iraq (2003), Indonesia (2005), the United Kingdom (2007) and Yemen

(2008). In addition, many other plots were foiled in various other countries around the globe. This increase can be explained by the fact that suicide terrorism is a smart bomb at the low expense for modern terrorists - a product of radical ideology with a modus operandi easily exportable and imitable.

Rational or Irrational

I strongly disagree with what some experts stated about the irrationality of suicide attacks because the rationality of these attacks has provided strong evidence in those countries that were or still are facing these deadly attacks. Among these countries are Israel, Iraq, Afghanistan and Pakistan, Indonesia, India, Russia and other countries. This phenomenon of suicide terrorism is not a new to the world, but this tactic is an old phenomenon practiced by radical Islamists since it started in Israel, Sri Lanka, and the USA, the UK and other countries. Israel is the only country who had faced a very high quantity of suicide attacks in the second Intifada. From 2000 to 2005, there were around 147 suicide attacks carried out against the state of Israel by Hamas and other Palestinian terrorist organisations. These attacks caused the deaths of more than 500 Israelis, the overwhelming majority were civilians. These suicide attacks were extremely lethal and the impacts of these attacks on the victim's population left a high grade of fear and panic among them.

These figures were successful suicide attacks only, around 450 suicide attacks were foiled on various stages by the Israeli security forces. These 147 suicide attacks were carried out by 156 Palestinian males and 8 females. It is essential to understand that suicide attacks are always carried out by organisations not by individual lone wolves. The main reason that suicide terrorism is growing is that terrorists have learned that it works. These attacks are initiated, planned, ordered and launched by the organisation. These attacks are not personally initiated but are organised attacks.

Committing suicide attacks are the outcome of rational decision processes because of their costs and what they consider as benefits. The terrorist organisation always gets multiple benefits to carry out suicide attacks against the state.

> ➢ To achieve the political goal

> ➢ The cost of attacks is very cheap

> ➢ Less chances of capturing a suicide bomber

> ➢ Lethality of attacks

> ➢ To spread more fear and panic among the victims

> ➢ Media attention

> ➢ To deliver a message to the local and international community

Suicide attacks are very advanced rational terrorist tactics compared to other tactics like shooting, stabbing, remote bombing, etc. Suicide terrorism is rational behaviour for both, the organisations and for the perpetrator himself. There are many examples of a famous organisation that have carried out suicide attacks and the LTTE was the most popular terrorist organisation that not only carried out suicide attacks against the state but also introduced the latest and most modern suicide tactics.

LTTE was the only organisation whose member were not caught by the security forces because they kept poison pills and swallowed then once they were arrested before being interrogated. Suicide attacks don't only occur against the occupation, but also against the Shia, Sunni and Saudi Arabian rulers.

I agree with argument stated by Dr Ganor that suicide attacks are more lethal and cause more casualties than any other type of bombing attacks. In suicide attacks, the perpetrator can control of the timing and the location of the incident and once he finds that a certain location does not have enough people at the time he has chosen, he can change the timing and placement whenever and wherever he wishes. This tactic of suicide attack proves that it is more rational than any other type of terrorist tactic.

I also agree with Dr Ganor that suicide terrorism is the most dangerous modus operandi of modern terrorism. There is a big difference between remote bombing and suicide bombing because in remote bombing, the timing and placement is not under the control of the perpetrator, but in suicide attack both the timing and placement are completely under control of the perpetrator this's why the lethal way of suicide terrorism is more dangerous than remote bombing.

According to the Robert Pape: "Most suicide terrorism is undertaken as a strategic effort directed toward achieving particular political goals; it is not simply the product of irrational individuals or an expression of fanatical hatreds" The aim of counterterrorism experts and pundits researching the field to counter a terrorist act successfully this's why we need to understand and know the terrorist's rational tactics, motivations, and ideologies and root cause. If such a thing does not exist and we believe that suicide bombers are irrational and crazy in every way, then why should we evaluate the grounds of their suicidal acts? So, I strongly believe that suicide terrorism is a rational act and there is solid ideology, reason, motivation and root cause for carrying out these lethal acts.

Root Causes

Suicide terrorism has the same root cause as any type of terrorism and there are many root causes but a unique root cause is to achieve a political goal. The other root causes behind suicide terrorism are as follows:

➢ Personal Motives / Motivations

➢ Religious obligation

- ➤ Huge benefits (worldly and hereafter)

- ➤ Brutal Occupation

- ➤ Political Goals

- ➤ Identity Issues

- ➤ Individual/ Psychological approach

Some experts argue that suicide terrorists are always against the brutality of the occupying state or the cruel treatment of their own democratic governments, but I believe these cases are not primary amongst suicide terrorist but the motivations, religious obligations and huge benefits are the main root causes behind it. For example, according to Dr. Ganor, "The factor that is most influential to Muslims who commit suicide attacks is religious beliefs. Religion unites most of the suicide attackers in the world and almost all the Muslim Shahids (Global and local Jihadi terrorists, the Palestinians, home grown terrorists, Chechens, Iraqis, etc.)"

This is one of the main root causes of suicide terrorism, the origins of suicide terrorism are not social or economic, brought on by humiliation or state terror, but rather by the religious, political-ideological characteristics of a population that support the use of suicide acts.

Suicide terrorism is more religious and cultural than political. It's rooted in religious teachings which provide the religious motivations and the justifications to get worldly benefits and dignity hereafter. The definition of suicide terrorism, which Dr Ganor accepted, "A suicide attack is an operational method in which the very act of the attack is dependent upon the death of the perpetrator" The suicide bomber is a rational actor, he knows and fully understand what he is going to do and fully agrees to carry out suicidal tactics to provide comprehensive benefits and obtain multiple objectives.

> ➤ Benefits to the religion

> ➤ Benefits to the organisation

> ➤ Benefits to the family

> ➤ Benefits to him/herself

> ➤ Benefits to the community

> ➤ Benefits to the state (state that provides suicide terrorist to gain political goals)

If we look at the benefits and motivations that drag someone to become a suicide bomber, we can understand that religious motivations are greater than the political or economic motivations. Terrorist organisations consider suicidal missions as successful tools to easily achieve a political goal. Through suicidal missions, they can create fear and anxiety for the victim nation and this pressurises the state to take weak action which means that terrorist organisations attain the political ends. Terrorist organisations always use suicide tool to carry out suicide attack because they prefer death than to life and being a martyr is their religious motivation. According to the Hezbollah leader Hasan Nasrallah: "We are going to win because they love life and we love death" Dr Ganor explained this situation very well and he stated: This is a unique situation in which the terrorist is fully aware that if he does not kill himself, the planned attack will not be carried out." How to describe the suicide attack, according to Martha Crenshaw: "Acts of terrorism that require the death of the perpetrator for successful implementation, typically known as "suicide" attacks"

One point I must make here is that the perpetrator of a suicidal act does not think he is committing a suicide but rather making himself a "Shahid" in Arabic. They believe that whoever becomes Shahid by committing suicide tactic will go to Jannah (paradise).

According to Dr Ganor, "The radical Islamic activists who decide to become "Shahids" see themselves as martyrs who are fulfilling a divine command of protecting their religion from the attack by the infidels". Terrorist acts usually emanate from rational, calculated, conscious decisions. These decisions represent an optimal strategy to attain the social–political goals of these perpetrators. Terrorism might not represent pathological or illogical behaviour but could represent the best means to fulfil personal needs in some circumstances. I believe that terrorists are quite rational and simply by considering how much time they spend on planning. They don't just appear suddenly and decide to attack something or somebody but rather they analyse the entire situation and decide where to start from. They decide what the outcomes might be both positive and negative and some of them also work out a plan "B" in case their initial strategy might fail.

This is why I believe terrorist are rational beings. They believe it is a part of a mechanism that is linked to some ideological ideas. Suicide Terrorism is rational behaviour, making suicide bombers rational actors who kill others to achieve certain goals. From the (Social) psychological approach, there is more or less consensus that they are not mentally unbalanced. According to Jerrold M Post, "Terrorists are not depressed and not severely emotionally disturbed, nor are they crazed fanatics. In fact, terrorist groups and organisations regularly weed out emotionally unstable individuals as they represent a security risk". Terrorists think about costs and benefits and think that violence is the best way to elevate their cause.

Motivations

The difference between a suicide attack and other attacks is the lethality. Suicide attacks are more lethal than normal terrorist attacks. The impact of a suicide attack is more dangerous because the result of a suicide attack causes more casualties than a normal attack. Suicide attacks cannot be carried out by individuals, but by an organisation. An organisation can choose where and when to send suicide bombers. The suicide attack is a more developed type of attack. In normal terrorist attacks, there are more chances for a terrorist to be caught on the spot and in a suicide attack it is less likely that a suicide member will be arrested. The terrorist organisation who carries out a suicide attack achieves many goals and two of them are most important.

> Instant Media Attention

> Fear and anxiety

Because a suicide attack is a more lethal attack than normal bombings the media keeps focused on this attack and though there are more casualties it generates more fear, horror and anxiety within targeted communities. I agree with the definition of the suicide bomber, according to Ariel Merari: "A situation in which a person intentionally kills himself (or herself) for the purpose of killing others in the service of a political or ideological goal" There are many motives, grievances and benefits behind a suicide bomber.

> Religious motives

> Personal motives

> Economic motives

> Political and nationalist motives

> Sociological Motives

According to Merari, "Suicide bombers can be driven by desires and emotions primarily focused on their private lives, with no or little connection with a collective, religious or political cause."

Religious motives are the most common factors for suicide attacks because in this cause suicide bombers get many personal and family or social worldly benefits.

Suicide is prohibited in most religions of the world, for example, Islam, Christianity and Judaism but if someone kills others and himself to get the higher religious reward, it is not considered as a suicide but a Martyrdom. Suicide bombers have a belief that once they commit a suicide mission, they will get 70 virgins hereafter and his family will get worldly honour within the community and they will be known very well among their people. In their (bombers) thoughts, they are not only serving for the nation or the country, but also protecting the religion as well by committing a suicide mission. According to Robert Pape, "Suicide terrorist is weaker actor target is the stronger"

Terrorist organisations always use suicide tactics when they know they are weaker than the target and cannot achieve a political goal. Modern terrorism is the phenomenon of psychological warfare that creates anxiety within the population. The psychological impact of terrorism is more fearful than any other form of attacks because victims become psychologically disabled and cannot react instantly.

The main goal of terrorists is to generate the terror which transfers people from rational fear into irrational fear. Terrorists want to generate irrational fear and panic in the hearts and minds of the ordinary citizens of the state. In this situation, our main policy should be, thwart the irrational fear which terrorists create within a targeted population. The outcome of The Shefayyim Conference is to educate the media on how to react when a terrorist incident occurs. At this conference, Dr Ganor discussed how certain types of media coverage of terror attacks do more damage to public morale than benefit the public's desire for new and important information. The targeted population must be educated so that terrorists cannot fulfil their goal of generating fear and anxiety within civilian populations. The reaction that people have of terrorist attack must be changed by the media and the media could play an important role in changing the psychological warfare atmosphere.

Some of the primary aims of The Shefayyim Conference are as below:

> Terrorism is designed to sap the moral strength of Israeli citizens and upset their way of life. In its threats and harmful onslaught on persons and property, terrorism causes moral and psychological damages.

> Terrorist attacks are meant to attain political aims-- change policies and influence political moves. To attain these aims, terrorism seeks broad media exposure, in order to reach various target populations and spread fear and anxiety.

> All agencies involved in the shaping of public opinion in Israel must contribute their share to the minimization of the moral-psychological damages of terrorism (including politicians, public figures, media people, academics, educators, etc.).

> Methods and guidelines must be formulated that will, on the one hand, enable the media to go on playing their crucial role in a democratic society of reporting freely and without external interference and, on the other hand, restrict the extent of the damages to people's sense of personal safety and to public morale.

The source of terror the likelihood that a terror – incident is going to occur again; the project of primary victimization (e.g. A member of one's family or one's group) and one's relationship to it. The phasing of the terror-producing event (single-phase incident like a massacre or duel phase incident like a hostage taking where the outcome is open ended but likely to be dreadful). One's (in) ability to avoid, prevent and combat which are terror-porn in the future.

Many people have had personal experiences of terrorist attacks in their lives, regardless of where they live. For example, if a suicide attack were to happen tomorrow on Times Square, New York, one of the first things to cross a person's mind would be: "I was just there 3 weeks ago; my family lives there; or, I was planning on going there. It is natural for people in the targeted population to personalise an attack, and this is precisely one of the primary aims of the terrorist organisations". While statistically, it is far more likely that a person can be hurt in a car accident on Times Square in New York than a by a suicide attack (even if one attack occurred there), the personalisation of an attack spreads irrational anxiety. Nevertheless, it is an innate human reaction for people to personalize an attack. Once a person is aware of natural trap and dangerous feeling of the personalisation of a terrorist attack, he might behave more rationally and the anxiety of terrorism might be limited.

Training & Recruitment

There are many phases for suicide terrorism and one of the main phases is training with modern tactics. Hezbollah and LTTE are among those organisations who are highly skilled in providing fully tactfully tactical training to create a suicide terrorist. Terrorist organisations do not always recruit candidates specifically for the suicide bombings but for the introduction of basic military training like Hezbollah and Hamas does. Counter Suicide Terrorism expert Mr. Ami Pedahzur explained this as, "A comparative appraisal of the training processes among the different organisations reveals an interesting picture. The majority of the terrorist organisations do not recruit candidates specifically for the suicide missions, and consequently preliminary training processes involve a combination of an introduction to basic military techniques and ideological- in many cases, religious-indoctrination." Hezbollah is the first terrorist organisation to have launched a suicide bomber and suicide bomber was the first to develop a two-stage training program for a suicide mission.

> ➤ Knowledge on how to prepare suicide mission

➤ Conduct the training process of suicide mission

The second largest suicide terrorism organisation was LEET, which had very close ties with Hezbollah in improving suicide techniques and also adopted their training methods. The LTTE had very sophisticated training methods for their suicide cadets and every new recruiter in the LTTE, most of whom were young children, had to go through a basic suicide training program for four months. In this primary training, they received an introduction to military tactics and an indoctrination in the organisation's ideology. The LTTE used many methods in training centres on a daily basis and they taught different tactics which they could use in a confrontation with the Army and security forces. According to the Ami Pedahzur, "A daily routine at LTTE camps began with an early wake-up call at 5 a.m. The children then underwent two hours of physical training in the jungle, followed by lessons in the martial arts. In the afternoon they attended classes, where they were introduced to the history of organisation and the Tamil people. Evenings were mostly devoted to classes in intelligence gathering and the handling of explosive devices."

There are many organisations which use suicide tactics to carry out successful suicide missions against the state to destabilise the democratic system. The Taliban, Al –Qaeda, Hamas, Hezbollah, LTTE, PKK and Chechen groups are the main organisations which are famous for using suicide tactics. These group training camps were located in different countries, for example, Hezbollah was trained in Iran, but later they established their own training camps in the Beqqa valley in Lebanon, with the help of Iranian officers. The Syrian army has a strong influence with the people of the Beqqa valley because the population of the valley is mostly Shiite. The Taliban had their own camps in Afghanistan, which were opened during the period of Afghan Soviet war and some are in the tribal areas of Pakistan. Hamas uses training camps in different countries, they first used them in Iran with the help of

Hezbollah, then in Lebanon and now mostly they provide their training in the Gaza area.

The largest LTTE training camps were located at Kolathur which is 11 kilometers from the Mettur Dam in the Salem district. The PKK is the Kurdish terrorist organisations and it fights for independence from the Turkish government. Its training camps, mostly were located in Syria, Lebanon and northern Iraq and the last Chechens terrorist group camps were Georgia and Pakistan.

Mr. Ami Pedahzur further highlighted this issue, "According to Russian intelligence sources, many Chechen rebels made use of the infrastructure of Mujahidin training camps in Georgia and Pakistan." There are many psychological programs provided by the terrorist organisations for the trainee suicidal cedars. For example:

➢ Showing them movies

➢ Telling them stories of brutality of the state

➢ Grievances

➢ Luring them with pictures

It's been recorded that some organisations used to drug the women in the process of mental preparation and this information is on the record by the female suicide bombers who were detained and interrogated by the governmental security forces.

Mr. Ami Pedahzur drew attention to this issue, "....... The period of grooming female potentials for suicide mission was in fact minimal and lasted around two weeks during which they became acquainted with basic tactics......... However, there are several testimonies who claimed that they have been drugged during the mental preparation process. Others maintained that they had been whipped up into an ecstatic frenzy. The described how they were taken into the large rooms where they were ordered to repeat a sentence over and over again and move their bodies in monotonous motions until they lost control......." The suicide bombers are widely available for sale in Pakistan, there were many incidents when suicide bombers were hired. According to the Police's Crime Investigation wing, "Anyone could buy a suicide bomber in $15,000 from WANA (Tribal) area".

It is reported that there are about 150 training camps in the tribal areas of Pakistan, where about 50,000 suicide terrorists are waiting for further instructions to carry out suicide missions within the country. The cost of availability for the personnel who carry out suicide mission is very cheap in tribal regions of Pakistan. *A Pakistani English newspaper reported:* "The Quetta police announced the arrest of 11 children who were allegedly involved in a series of bomb explosions. The teenaged suspects' ages ranged from 11 to 18, and they all came from poor families. Police claimed the teenagers were responsible for more than one dozen bomb explosions and that terrorists paid them 2,000 to 5,000 rupees ($19 to $47) per bombing" Terrorists use the tactic of kidnaping adult people for the ransom, but they also kidnap young children to use as spies, fight and suicide missions. They use those children as child soldiers to achieve their goals.

According to the Country's Human Rights Report, "Nonstate militant groups kidnapped boys and girls and used fraudulent promises to coerce parents into giving away children as young as age 12 to spy, fight, or die as suicide bombers. The militants sometimes offered parents' money, often sexually and physically abused the children, and used psychological coercion to convince the children that the acts they committed were justified." According to the independent research website, "There were about suicidal incidents happened in Pakistan, which caused more than 6,000 deaths from 2001 to 2015."

These suicidal terrorist incidents have been carried out in Pakistan, more than any other country around the world. Israel is the first victim of suicide terrorism incidents after Pakistan, however, there have been more than 600 suicide attacks on the soil of Israel and more than 450 suicide attacks have been foiled successfully by the Israeli security forces. So, quantity wise, Israel is the country that has been affected by suicide terrorism.

Suicide Terrorism effects among victims

The effects of suicide terrorism are very intense for the entire nation of the victim country. People not only suffer from different types of fear and anxiety, but the psychological effect of terrorism remain in the country for a long time. There are many types of effects which completely ruined the lives of victims of terrorism. Here are some of them:

- Emotional Effects
- Cognitive Effects
- Physical Effects
- Interpersonal Effects

So apart from, above there are many other common symptoms which disturb the victim's daily routine system.

- Feeling helpless
- Detachment and Numbness
- Disturbed and Startled
- Unsecure feelings
- Nightmare and trouble sleeping
- Feeling lazy and unhappy at the workplace and home
- Develops a fear psychosis
- Uncertainty of future
- Mistrust for the law of the land
- Helplessness as an individual

> ➤ Increase stress and anxiety

> ➤ Incites hatred or violence against individual or group

> ➤ Increase aggression

> ➤ Strengthen the belief that violence is the last solution

Some people are more affected by a traumatic event than others, it totally depends on the nature of the event and the nature of the individual's experience of the situation.

The victims of suicide terrorism or common terrorism are suffering from Posttraumatic stress disorder (PTSD). The symptoms, PTSD have many psychological, emotional, social and physical effects. According to the American Psychiatric Association: PTSD is a mental disorder resulting from exposure to an extreme, traumatic stressor. PTSD has a number of unique defining features and diagnostic criteria. Further stated that these criteria, including Exposure to a traumatic stressor - Re-experiencing symptoms - Avoidance and numbing symptoms - Symptoms of increased arousal- Duration of at least one month- significant distress or impairment of functioning. The victims or survivors of terrorism are at high risk of a range of PTSD problems. These people are direct witnesses or survivals of any kind of terrorism, especially suicide terrorism. There are some survivors who have a high risk of Post disasters: 1- Exposure of mass destruction of death, family or friend 2- Sudden or violent death of a loved one 3- Loss of home or community 4- Loss of land or business or sudden unemployment 5- Property destruction 6- Personal Injury.

When terrorist attacks occur, children may witness or learn about them on TV, talking to people at school and by hearing from adults who are discussing the terror events. Children are affected more easily than adults because of their young age and they remember many things that are happening around them and it has a negative effect on their minds. Research shows that children of any age are strongly affected by terrorist incidents. A few days after 9/11, a survey showed that 35% parents said that their children have some kind of stress due to the terrorist attack.

Almost half of them reported that their children were worried about their own safety, or the safety of their loved one.

This was an important finding because these children were not direct victims or witnesses of any sort of terrorism or had any relation with the people were killed or injured, but they had just read or watched the terror attack in the newspaper or on TV. Parents have a great responsibility to teach their children positively and let them know about reality and be prepare them for any event that might happen should not only look after them but take care of their parents as well by providing positive reassurance. According to the National centre for PTSD: Although providers and parents may be anxious or scared, children need to know that attacks are rare events. Children also need to know that the world is generally a safe place. I have tried my best to provide all sorts of information about suicide terrorism, their tactics and effects and still it needs a lot of research and practical work to highlight latest suicide tactics because each day new suicidal techniques are introduced. More work is needed to stop this lethal bloody game around the world and this is how to Ami Pedahzur described the situation:

The devastating nature of suicide terrorism has multiplied the effect of terrorism on individuals, societies and political systems, and thus created a grave, new and immediate challenge for many societies. In his paper about suicidal individuals, Dr. Alex. Lickerman provided six reasons why people commit suicide:

1. They're depressed. This is without question the most common reason people commit suicide. Severe depression is always accompanied by a pervasive sense of suffering as well as the belief that escape from it is hopeless.

2. They're psychotic. Malevolent inner voices often command self-destruction for unintelligible reasons.

3. They're impulsive. Often related to drugs and alcohol, some people become maudlin and impulsively attempt to end their own lives.

4. They're crying out for help, and don't know how else to get it. These people don't usually want to die but do want to alert those around them that something is seriously wrong.

5. They have a philosophical desire to die. The decision to commit suicide for some is based on a reasoned decision, often motivated by the presence of a painful terminal illness from which little to no hope of reprieve exists.

6. They've made a mistake. This is a recent, tragic phenomenon in which typically young people flirt with oxygen deprivation for the high it brings and simply go too far.

If you examine the rationale for suicidal terrorism, reason number 2 and 5 fits the justification for suicide bombers. One of the reasons or the main reason we have heard people offered themselves as suicide bomber, is the belief that they will go to heaven and have seven virgins. This relates to a psychotic state of mind, who is hearing inner voices commanding them to self-destruct, and so they become suicide bombers. Number 5 is based on the ideology of the terrorist group, the suicide bombers believes that their personal or political grievance will never be addressed due to their inferior, suffering and weak position against a powerful nation. Therefore, choose to kill themselves by deciding to become a suicide bomber.

The main reason we have heard people offered themselves as a suicide bomber, is the belief that they will go to heaven and have seven virgins. This relates to a psychotic state of mind, who is hearing inner voices commanding them to self-destruct, and so they become suicide bombers.

Chapter 4

No Media -No Terrorism

"The publicity (Media) is the oxygen of Terrorism"

-Ex- British PM Margareta Thatcher

Media coverage of terrorist groups in the Islamic world is unrealistic and lengthy than the impact of the events. Media all around the world helped terrorists to glorify their actions and get fresh recruitment within youth. Media needs to reorganise all news hour coverage based on human and physical impact of any event instead emotional impact.

The media needs to pay more attention to accuracy, it seems in a rush to be the first to "break a story" they are willing to sacrifice accuracy. Many members of the media don't consider the repercussions of certain sometimes vital information reaching certain people, a lack of responsibility. Hiding behind the freedom of the press some act smugly, almost cocky as if there is no responsibility attached to freedom, no accountability. I by no means am directing my comments at all or even most members of the media. In fact, it is a small minority, they are just impossible to ignore.

This subject is of mass conjecture. Should the media report it or not? We live, mostly in a world of free speech and the terrorist groups have made maximum use of this. The terrorist's goal is to seek mass publicity, in order to gain recruits, glamorise their aims, and thus gain their aim of mass terror. The London 7/7 bombings highlighted the use of the media as they were reporting of the attacks in mere minutes. On a more, terrible note, the torching of the Jordan pilot alive, was basically of a "Hollywood" style production, filmed in and edited. It was then posted on you-tube, Twitter, Facebook and other social Internet sites as well as the TV, a very professional production! The media is there as to report all over the globe. Free media is a very cheap costly way of promoting and radicalising people from around the world. If we start to stop coverage of the media where will it end? with the state saying what you can publish, it's the free state we live in, that gives the terrorists its course of mass media terror.

After watching several interviews, videos of terrorist groups on different private and government owned media houses, I can say for sure, that this helps big time in the free advertisement of terrorism. Whether unwitting but a grave mistake made by every media house. If culprit's intention is to reach to the masses, and by showing their messages even if for the sake of awareness fulfils their purpose. Some experts argue that they are more disciplined in their line of work, as compare to the state and their actors. Even some counter terrorism pundits urge governments should ban all kind of media coverage to these terrorist groups, their filthy attacks, their mind-set anything that represent their agenda at all.

I agree with the principle that the terrorists have too much media coverage. Whether television, newspapers, social media or even the web in general, the terrorist uses of media technology to spread their propaganda and media Westerners aid. People surely viewed the latest videos of ISIS, they will spread like a virus around the world. I do not say that I am for the censorship of media, but I say that a minimum of common sense would not do them from wrong. Whenever the media rebroadcast a video of terrorists, they are both complicit because media facilitate the propagation. Terrorist groups are rendered with sections dealing with public relations and propaganda. They are no longer the uneducated have believed.

The interaction between the media and terrorist has intensified because of the increase in available information and around-the-clock news coverage. According to Piers Robinson "CNN, with its global reach, 24-news cycle and foreign affairs agenda, came to encapsulate the idea of a media- driven foreign policy, sometimes known as the "CNN effect". The media should pay more attention to accuracy, based on the governmental media policy.

In world's different regions have different media phenomenon but the complaint is the same of media under-reporting events especially terrorist events, often their reports do not actually reflect the true picture of what is going on but the baffling experience is that reverse is the case when reporting the terrorist side of the story. Surprisingly Dr. Juliet Bird (Head of CT, NATO HQ) stated in one of her lectures delivered in University of Maryland USA in Jan 2015 and she stated "NATO rely on information by journalists in the alliance state"

If I am not mistaken, this means that they only rely on what they are been told apart from observing from afar, how are they sure they are been fed accurately of turn of events. The high advance in use of technology I think has made it possible for terrorist to easily post whatever they want to the public of which most times the media houses get the information on net themselves. For example, the ongoing insurgent in Nigeria from time to time you see various videos of killings and torture of Military officers by Boko Haram members posted on YouTube which in most cases are not reported by media. And the physical ones they are opportune to witness will not be accurately reported. I think the media should look into the mode of censorship of news to at least reflect the true picture of whatever is happening.

One of the interesting things we must learn about the Caliphate, which should be the world centre for Muslims. The media has not provided this education for people to understand the background of Islam in connection to terrorism. What we see in the media are pundits simply talking past one another. The media has focus more on the spectacle of terrorist's violence than providing well balance and objective reporting that informs and educate rather than entertain. According to Martha Crenshaw "Terrorism is more a threat to image and reputation than to physical security."

There are many critical matters, States have to consider very seriously and Media is one of them. The role of media, especially in the incidents of terrorism, their information, disinformation, their coverage and usage, these all things are very closely countable when it operates. The impacts of media terrorism are psychologically rooted in the minds of population. There are many countries and few of them have strictly controlled the media according to introducing the tougher media laws.

The main countries of them, are Israel, Russia, China and Saudi Arabia. Israel had the same problem as Pakistan have but since Israel introduced tougher media laws and the negative impact of media on public became lowered. One thing I highlight here that before making tougher laws Israel called over all media owners and their senior experts and showed them actual facts and figures. Israeli media realised that if they did not change their pattern, terrorists may win the hearts of a nation. This is one of the other options to make media owners realise that they are psychologically playing in the hands of terrorists.

It would be challenging to properly situate projection, in the form of media defence mechanism for promoting terrorist organisations. I think the media has not really been mad at terrorist organisations but kind of enjoying the violence in a sadistic manner. I will attempt to say that the media should be covering the general human events of ordinary people, in the homeland of terrorist organisation. Instead of depicting the adventures and military exploits of terrorist organisations, riding in armour vehicles, in capture areas. The media should be covering the tragic of human suffering, as a result of terrorist attacks, not covering how much strength a terrorist organisation has gained. According to Peter Krause "At the tactical level of effectiveness, terrorism is designed to kill people, kill civilians, destroy infrastructure and inspire fear."

This is the message that must be echoed from a different viewpoint, not from terrorist leaders demonstrating their gains on the battlefield of death. The coverage of terrorism in themes of "heroic efforts, and sacrifice honour for the greater good" feeds into the terrorist strategy, to induce cognitive opening, for acceptance to redress political grievances. "Repetition and familiarity" of terrorist's combativeness and military readiness by the media can offer subliminal messages to potential lone wolves or inspire unstable minds to internalize terrorism as a positive tactic to address personal, social or political grievance.

Media has its own advantages and disadvantages, from one hand media`s role is important in letting people know about the current challenges in the world, people become more aware about the conflict areas in which they are being warned not to travel to and so on and so forth, but on the other hand media serves also as an inspiration or as an instruction note (like it was in the case of Inspire magazine and I was very impressed to see what they were publishing in this magazine).

Moreover, I never thought that media could also serve as a way to escape from police like it was in the case of the Mumbai attack, when terrorists actually used internet to communicate, GPS to escape and LIVE news to anticipate and counter police efforts, which was very interesting to hear. So, in a case like the Mumbai attack, should the media/internet/all sorts of network communication be stopped during such an event in order to prevent terrorists from escaping? According to the Washington Post "They carried BlackBerrys, CDs holding high-resolution satellite images like those used for Google Earth maps, and multiple cell phones with switchable SIM cards that would be hard to track. They spoke by satellite telephone. And as television channels broadcast live coverage of the young men carrying out the terrorist attack, TV sets were turned on in the hotel rooms occupied by the gunmen, eyewitnesses recalled"

The media places dual roles when it comes to terrorism. While it plays an important role in informing the world about the happenings, sometimes it tends to exaggerate and blow out of proportion the level of event and this gives advantage to the terrorist group which wants to instil fear and panic in viewer. Also, with the availability of social network at our finger tips, the media is easily accessible and terrorist groups have greatly used this to its advantage. The Inspire Magazine is a good example where individuals are called upon to act in the name of certain ideologies. Most of the foreign fighters involve in the war in Iraq and Syria involving ISIS or ISIL were recruited via the media. So, the media can be seen as a double-edged sword.

Another problem, while media plays an important role sometimes it tends to exaggerate and that exaggeration is useful for the perpetrators because the media is seen as a tool in spreading the propaganda. Not to mention about the Fox News which posted the video in which ISIS burned alive a Jordanian pilot and almost everybody criticised them for spreading the ISIS propaganda, calling the Fox News as "ISIS's PR"... "A new video that surfaced on the Internet appears to show ISIS burning alive a Jordanian pilot the terror group has held since December 2014."

For example, about the Inspire Magazine and the usefulness of the media in recruiting foreign fighters, I would like to say that I have read in the Central Asia forum that some states have temporary banned social networks because they considered these means of communication as very dangerous, so wouldn't a temporary ban on social networks be also useful for other states? It's true that Central Asia didn't prevent their citizens to join some groups as

I heard that poor people or uneducated people are joining ISIS, however I assume that these citizens didn't join them when the media was blocked and I believe that people would not have joined ISIS if the propaganda wouldn't have been spread in those countries.

Some experts on counter terrorism comment about the importance of the "gold hour" regarding the media after a terrorist attack. According to their idea, the population has to be informed, even if there is still incomplete information, with a message avoiding emotional content as soon as possible. Better to inform partially and honestly of the information available than not to communicate anything and allow rumours spread all around creating uncontrolled fear. I guess there are specific policies about this of course including the kind of vocabulary to transmit the message.

I agree that the population has to be informed especially if an attack has been taking place in a specific country so people could avoid those areas, however, wouldn't be better to inform only about the place where the attack occur and skip the information about which roots should be followed in order to avoid the regions? Because the perpetrators would use that information to escape... wouldn't be better to provide only a fast warning? And only after the attackers have been caught then the media could provide more information about what actually happened, who was responsible and so on...? Media is an important instrument in disseminating helpful information, yet the media is a double edge sword. Most terrorist organisations rely on media courage to spread its propaganda: provocation, attraction, spoil, outbidding or intimidation. The aim of terrorist organisations is to instate fear through intimidation. Without media courage, a terror organisation will not be able to have global propaganda publicity.

Terrorism cannot be understood from a single discipline. Therefore, as a case study let view terrorism from a marketing point of view. Let assume Isis is a new company trying to market a product name "fear". But before Isis markets its product (fear), Isis also has to make itself a name brand. Hence, to became a brand name and market its product Isis needs media-advertisement: The more a product is advertising, the more it is promoted, the more it's become known, it raises demographics' awareness as well as educate people of related benefits of the product and services. My point is that, in as much as we need the media to educate us on the activities of a terrorist organisation, it is also important that the media understand the fine line between educating the public and promoting the terrorist organisation. Terrorist organisations need media attention as a source of advertising the fear it wishes to instead, while at the same time promoting its brand (the name of the terrorist organisation), for the purpose of mobilisation and recruitment.

There should be a delay between when a major event happens and when the media can release certain information. Regularly when an incident is live, they take information from the internet and social media, such as Twitter or Facebook. An unofficial source being used as a reference often leads to false information. A recent example of this is back in October 2014 when a shooter stormed Parliament Hill in Ottawa, Canada. All the major news agencies reported up to three shooters, two of whom had barricaded themselves in a mall. This was based on Twitter posts. It turns out there was only one shooter and he was nowhere near the mall. In addition, the information the media puts out there can be used by terrorists or other bad guys to their advantage. The media saying, "this road is blocked off by police so drive on this road instead" can provide an escape route, etc.

Media is often wrongly portraying a specific situation. So the media could provide false information, it can be also used as propaganda, it can provide escape root for perpetrators, it is seen as a means to counter police efforts, it is often used as a means to recruit foreign fighters, it can be also used as an instruction "book" for people who want to build a weapon or instructions on how they can take action and media sometimes is publishing only one version of a story or only one state's view and not both states views (states which are in conflict)... if we put this in a balance the disadvantages are bigger than the advantages.

Terrorists are taking seriously the consequences of their attacks and especially the possibility of attracting media, in order to achieve their socio-political or other goals. Terrorism and media are having a very special relationship. Terrorism successes and failures are based a lot on publicity and propaganda. Terrorist attacks outweigh the daily news, while the emphasis that is given on dramatic news, functions not only for terrorists but also for the political leadership and government as well. On the other side, the media side, the creation of images, of terrorism spectacles, the interpretation of terrorist issues and its influence on the public are strongly in times of crisis.

The media should cover terrorism objectively, without fear or favour. If anything, the media coverage of terrorism has been very controversial depending on which divide they belong. This condition, in my humble view, has progressively and increasingly expanded terrorism both domestically and internationally. The media is either over-reporting or under-reporting, depending on where, who and how it perceives the attack. By this manner of coverage, the media impact how we think terrorist attacks are carried out. For example, the over-reaction that accompanied high profile attacks like 9/11, Madrid 3/11, London 7/7, Mumbai attack and the attack in Paris was obviously a sharp contrast to the under-reporting of the alleged massacre of over 2000 people in Baga, Nigeria.

Despite the shortcomings of the media, I think the Government should still relate with them, by utilising their open source information, though with extreme caution. Generally, I think the media coverage of terrorism, especially in the third world countries have done more harm than good to counter terrorism.

Terrorism has to be countered from all the statements of the society, and the media play an important role in this.

They have a main role to create resilience in the society, providing objective information and avoiding extra-fear. This is critical and not easy to do. For this reason, they are necessary pre-established policies to achieve this between the different actors (media, government, police, etc...). The experience from the past in some countries maybe has not been positive, but it is a continuous learning process and probably today this issue is better than in the past although there is still room from improvement.

In most of the discussions involving the media and terrorism, it seems the media is viewed as a separate entity outside and isolated from the rest of us. This is not the case. The media is comprised of people, some with agendas perhaps, but still people, who live in society. They will have their personal feelings, yes, but they are simply doing a job. And what is there job? To report the news...to us. The media is going to report on the news its readers and viewers want to hear. Thus, in the US, people are not going to hear many news stories discussing the Tamil Tigers. People will hear a great deal about the Islamic State because it is in the Middle East and we have a perceived fear of the oil being adversely affected by an imbalance in the status quo. But the media is going to report what its readers want to read. We are the ones to blame for their choice of stories. We in the western world heard a great deal about Charlie Hebdo because it was of greater interest to us compared to the 2000 slaughtered by Boko Haram.

Media has a big challenge. They have to sell newspapers and magazines, or get enough viewers and subscribers. The best way to do this is, of course, to be exciting. Media are also supposed to report truthfully and honestly. Unfortunately, that doesn't always happen. There can be a lot of gray area in a story. How a particular new agency presents that story could make it "fair and balanced" or sensationalised. Media also cater to their audiences.

It is also a fair point that media attention may actually make terrorism worse because it calls attention to the events and lets future perpetrators know terrorism is a way to publicise their causes or just get people to pay attention to them. Maybe this is even more significant for lone wolves, some of whom are more unbalanced and potentially less strategic and deliberate in their thinking.

Partly I think the massacre in Baga, Nigeria was not well covered by the media for the reason I already mentioned before: the average person in the West does not immediately identify with people living in a small town in a remote area of Nigeria. But, even if the media had wanted to cover Baga better than it did, how would it? Can news agencies easily and safely get to Baga to report on the events that occurred there? Probably not. However, reporting from Sydney, Paris, and Copenhagen is fairly safe.

Media has a very important role to play in covering the terrorism. In my opinion media should play a very balanced and objective approach while covering the sensitive areas like terrorism. Because their small mistake, can lead to the exposure of the things that required some secrecy from the political and security point of view. Government and media should always be on the same lines as far as issues like terrorism is concerned. None should try to score points on each other as it is the question of the integrity of the country. At least till the time the operations are complete and all the correct information is available, no significant disclosures should be made public. The Media does hinder counter terrorism in some ways. Indeed, in the 70's and 80's in the UK certain IRA individuals were not given any publicity at all. Their images were blanked and their words were distorted in sound when they are given any coverage.

Media outlets are kind of like the magazine Inspire. The media outlets are in the 'businesses to make money, pass on information and to inspire individuals to continue to watch them. A bombing in sub-Saharan Africa or an attack by Boko Haram that kills 300 is given one-line notification, while the attack in Paris garners days of non-stop coverage. Not that either event is more or less significant, it is where can that particular media outlet has the biggest impact and gain. The problem with the media outlets is when, like Inspire, they move to one or the other end of the political spectrum and thus taint the actual event or information with the personal and institutional biases.

Terrorist organisations use media, for sure, to propagate their message--witness ISIS' recent videos and announcements that received much media attention. It is probably true that the terror organisations anticipate how the main stream media will respond to their releases and use that knowledge to "tailor" their message. I do not think that the media intentionally allow themselves to be used as the news outlet for terrorists, otherwise the only viewpoint presented about any given event would be that of the terrorists.

Media is a bi-directional communication channel. When ISIS released videos of a person burning in a cage, it is sending messages to its foes and its potential recruits. Different messages perhaps, but the channel is the same. When videos of drone strikes are released, the state actors are sending a message to ISIL and to their potential recruits. Different messages, but the same channel. So, this medium is transmitting messages in both directions.

If your use of "Media coverage" means formally organised entities such as the BBC or the New York Times, then the same applies, I believe. No independent reporters are going to survive being in-bedded with ISIS if they are truly objective. And the cost of maintaining reporters in far flung locations has reduced their use to near zero. So, traditional media is using press releases generated by the state actors for the most part. The use of the media is accomplished by all sides. There is little of no difference between media coverage and media usage. There is no media outlet that is purely objective, despite their claims. And, all sides will use the media to best spin their story, tailoring the message to the media outlet. More precisely, the media is nothing more than the vehicle used to convey the message to the masses.

This is what former TV News boss and award-winning journalist Adrian Monck said in his book: "The media dominates our lives. We give more time to viewing, surfing, listening and reading than we do to our families and friends. It's a relationship that's built on trust and it's a relationship currently in crisis. TV's fake phone-ins, phoney footage from royal reality shows, reporters resorting to phone-bugging to get stories - is there anything left in the media we can believe?"

As the U.S State Department definition states, "Terrorism is premeditated, politically motivated violence perpetrated against non-combatant targets by subnational groups or clandestine state agents, usually intended to influence an audience."

I personally like what Alexander I. Solzhenistyn says; "If only there were evil people somewhere insidiously committing evil deeds and it were necessary only to separate them from the rest of us and destroy them. But the line dividing good and evil cuts through the hearts of every human, and being, and who is willing to destroy a piece of his own heart?" I make a case from the perspective of the American media, and with deep hesitation, I argue the American media has become securitised for terrorism organisations, to influence responses to terrorism more than policy frameworks that addresses the fundamental grievances and other rational for terrorist's violence. The American media coverage of terrorism is more in the form of popular culture, creating an "us vs them" warfare and without differentiating terrorist organisations and their motivations. The media is also covering terrorism in a propaganda manner, as a response to extremist ideology, and creating a narrative that amplifies irrationality and madness of terrorist organisations, more so than reporting on objective facts and public diplomacy.

Chapter 5

The Threat of Islamic Extremism in the West

The world is currently suffering from the heat of terrorism all across the world. The seeds of terrorism arose in the Middle East in the 19th century, when Islamic rebellions called *Khawarij or Khawarijis attacked in the Muslims house of Allah in Mecca – Saudi Arabia in late70s. In the current days, Islamic extremism has risen from the Middle East in the 19th century but the Arab states and the Western countries did not bother them and took this rising threat minimum until it started destroying the Western civilisation and posed a direct threat to the Western democratic values.

*The Khawarij: The Modern-day Jihadist revolutionary groups are collectively known amongst early and later-day Muslim scholars as the Khawarijis. In Islamic terminology, the word refers to those who exit the rule of the one in authority over them. They refuse to accept his authority and rebel; most commonly under the pretext of the charge of disbelief and removing of injustice. Another term that has been used for them by the scholars and Jurists is Takfiris. The term takeover here refers to those who go to extremes in declaring Muslims to be apostate, disbeliever or an infidel.

In November 1979, a radical Islamic group stormed the Grand Mosque in Mecca, the most sacred city in Islam. They had been smuggling weapons into the mosque over the period of days under burial shrouds and clothing. The siege lasted twenty days and was led by a group who believed that they had amongst a just leader who is to appear at the end of time and who will remove the injustices of the rulers and establish the law of God. After twenty days, these Islamic terrorists were killed, captured and executed in the army operation. They were Khawarijis who wanted to top down the Kingdom of Saudi Arabia and attacked the Grand Mosque of Mecca and spread the blood of Muslim pilgrims.

In October 1981, the Egyptian president, Anwar Sadat was assassinated in Cairo by an extremist group calling itself Jama'at al-Jihad (their leaders later called merged into the Muslim Brotherhood), as he reviewed a parade commemorating in the 1973 war. Lieutenant Khalid Istambuli, the leader of the assassin carried out, "I am Khalid Istambuli, I have killed Pharaoh and I do not fear death".

In February 1982, local members of the Muslim brotherhood, Al-Ikhwan al-Muslimoon, founded in Egypt, instigated a rebellion in the Syrian town of Hama. The government forces moved in with air and ground attack and recaptured the area from the Islamic terrorist group, killed around 40,000 to 50,000 thousand of Hama residents and destroyed the city of Hama completely. There are various examples of these types of Islamic/Khawarij terrorist incidents in the Middle East and the Muslim and the Western world that are all too often ignored and forgotten, they have continued through onto the twenty-first century with devastating consequences for Muslims and non-Muslims in the world alike.

Over the two decades the United Kingdom and the West in general has seen a rise of Jihadist extremism. Radical groups using methods similar to those of cult sects, have substantially increased their recruitment of disaffected Muslims, especially focusing upon youths, vulnerable and convert to Islam. Muslims and non-Muslims alike need to understand the context within those extremist sects operate and the principles they have invented to propagate their dangerous ideology.

They must also understand the pretext they utilise to attacks target in the West. Indeed, suicide bombing, stabbing and car ramming in the West and in Israel is mare symptoms and extensions of that which these groups have unleashed upon the Muslim population for decades.

The extremists see the streets and markets of London, New York, Paris, Madrid, Karachi, Mumbai, Riyadh, Mecca and Jerusalem, to name a few, as "domains of war". The enemy is the established democratic government; the target for them is any person who happens to live within the domain of war, Muslims or non-Muslims alike. Their intent is to scare and shake democratic and peaceful societies, to create fear in civilian's faces, to put terror into the hearts of the victims' population, to destabilise elected governments; all of this is justified for them through Jihadist slogans, amongst which is "Whosoever does not judge by what Allah has revealed are the disbelievers".

Islam denounces any type of extremism, rebelliousness and mischief in religion and against the innocent people in the world. There are many Islamic texts that condemned extremism and extremists. Early day and later day Muslim scholars strongly condemned and warned of the mischiefs of the Khawarij (Jihadist Extremist) in the world, even though, the Prophet of Islam (Peace Be upon Him) warned in his sayings against the Khawarij groups.

The prophet of Islam (PBUH) stated: "Beware of extremism in religion, for that which destroyed those who came before was extremism in religion" "The extremists are destroyed. The extremists are destroyed. The extremists are destroyed."

The third-century Muslim scholar Ahmed bin Hanbal (RA) stated: "The Khawarijis are evil people. I do not know upon the earth a person a more evil than them. There authentic narrations from the Prophet concerning (their censure) from ten different aspects".

Ash-Shahrastani (RA) stated:

"They (Khawarij) speak with takfir of those who commits a major sin and they declare that he is in the hellfire eternally."

Ibn Taymiyyah (RA) stated: "The Khawarijis were the first to declare Muslims to be apostates; they would declare them to be disbelievers based upon sins that did not constitute idolatry.

They declared anyone who did not agree with them in their deviate innovation to be disbelievers and made permissible the shedding of their blood and forcibly taking their wealth."

In the current era, these Khawarijis run and operate their Jihadist activities under different Jihadi groups and names such as Al-Qaeda, ISIS, Taliban, The Muslims Brotherhood, Hamas, Hizb-ut-Tehrir, Bako Haram, Al-Muhajiroon and many others. The religious violent extremism exists in Islam and it is now clear that the Prophet of Islam (PBUH) informed his followers that extremism is a reality that will take place, and thus, Muslims ought to be aware and not be deceived by those radicals who say "There is no such thing as extremism and that there are no such divisions in Islam".

It is therefore incumbent upon every Muslim to free himself and distance himself from these rebellious Jihadist groups, regardless of what beautifully embellished title they give themselves.

Indeed, it is a collective duty of the Muslims to inform or any suspicious activity of someone, pass on any information they have about these Muslim Jihadists and hand to terrorists and even Jihadist sympathisers or extremists to the authorities in Muslim countries or even in non-Muslim/Western countries and this is not considered as a betrayal in Islam.

The UK Parliament attack, Prevent Policy and the UK Muslims Responsibility

March 22nd, 2016 was a devastating day in the UK for a lone wolf terrorist, a British born convert and ISIS sympathizer, rammed his car into people at the Westminster Bridge, killing a few and injuring around 40 people. He ran towards the UK Parliament, stabbed a Police Officer, killed him and was finally shot dead by other armed officers in order to prevent him from entering the UK Parliament. It was hard for people around the world to watch the live scenes of the Parliament attack. I have categorised this terror incident via three perspectives in this article in order to help one understand the terror wave in the United Kingdom.

Terror incident and terrorist's objectives

It was not an ordinary attack for an attack at a parliament is always considered as an attack on the country and an attack on the democracy of the United Kingdom, just as the attack on the Indian Parliament in 2001 was. ISIS finally attacked the heart of London at the British Parliament, which is a very shocking event in the history of the United Kingdom.

I saw this attack as a rehearsal for the terror organisation in order to assess the capabilities of the security services before carrying out a powerful attack in the UK, as they tried many times but our security forces foiled them before it happened. The prime objective of the terrorist was to generate fear and anxiety within the victim country and the attack on the British Parliament was a great challenge to the UK government for it shows that the terrorist is capable enough to damage the international credibility of the country and to destabilise the democratic system in the United Kingdom. ISIS successfully sent its message by conducting the terror attack, showing that the terrorist organisation is getting stronger through their sleeper cells within the Muslim community in the United Kingdom.

This attack is uniquely different from other terrorist attacks, which raises a serious question for the country's security institutions.

> ➤ There were two separate terrorist attacks at a time, a car ramming over people and the stabbing of a police officer at the Parliament.

> ➤ The two terrorist incidents were carried out by a single lone wolf attacker

> ➤ The terrorist's intention was to enter into the Parliament in order to harm others, which I consider to be an attempt to carry out a third terrorist incident intentionally

In my opinion, ISIS's goal was not to kill as many people as they could (if they get a chance) but was to challenge the authority of the UK's security capability. If their goal was to kill more people, they could have used other means to do so, such as suicide attack or by using firearms.

The UK's security departments need to work hard in order to prevent more terrorist incidents. The government needs to increase the number of police officers by recruiting thousands more and deploying in the capital city of the country. The UK government should not rely on electronic surveillance only and or on technical capabilities but must focus on human intelligence for only it can gather strong and effective Intel within the affected community.

UK's Prevent Policy

I am not a big fan of UK's prevent policy, which was made very soon after the 9/11 attacks but afterwards, the citizens of the UK faced a great terror menace in the shape of 7/7 underground train bombings. The counter terrorism experts are aware of four Ps which are the main pillars of the CONTEST (United Kingdom's Counter Terrorism) strategy, which was introduced in 2003 and was implemented in the public by 2006 just after 7/7 tragedy. The four Ps of the CONTEST strategy are **Prevent, Pursue, Protect** and **Prepare**. Here I am talking about preventing policy. I will not talk further about the other three Ps except to prevent because it is the main and basic policy which may deter the terrorism effectively.

The purpose of preventing terror is to stop people from becoming terrorists or supporting terrorism. This includes countering terrorist ideology and challenging those who promote it, support individuals who are especially vulnerable to becoming radicals and working with sectors in institutions where the risk of Radicalisation is assessed to be high.

Now let's see how the prevent policy really prevented someone from becoming a potential extremist or terrorist? After 2003 or let's talk about when they officially implemented it, which is a year after 7/7 bombing in 2006, there were thousands of people who became Radicalised and joined local and international terrorist cells. There is an official report that nearly 600 British Muslims who travel to Syria and Iraq joined the ISIS terror group but according to an unofficial report compiled by the security think tanks, the actual number of extremists who travelled outside the country in order to join international terrorist organisations was over 2,000.

Every year, local Muslims are becoming extremists rapidly and there is not any powerful tool in place in order to stop them from becoming Radicalised. We don't have a strong policy to monitor mosques, Madrasahs and local community centres. We do not have enough checks and balances to surveillance effectively. The governments prevent department strongly needs a comprehensive surveillance policy with a proper and fair checks and balances based on human intelligence. The public is losing their trust in the security services to provide comprehensive security and safety. People pay huge taxes and they have a right to have their lives, limbs and property protected.

The British Muslim's role in the society

British Muslims have a great a role in stabilizing the country economically and to take part in a democracy respectively. Ninety nine percent of British Muslims are officially declared as law abiding citizens. However, one percent of the Muslims are supporting international terrorism, which is a really worrying thing in the country. These one percent black sheep within the Muslim community not only blackened the name of the entire religion but disgrace the peaceful Muslim community in Great Britain. Unfortunately, the positive and proactive role of the Muslim community in order to deter extremism and radicalisation is non-existent. Everyone knows, these extremists are using the places of worship (Mosques and Madrasahs) and local community centres for their dirty political Islamist ideology and the leadership of the religious and secular communities are completely failing to identify the cancer of Islamism within them.

The silent protest of the local Muslim community is their major mistake and extremists are using their silence as a strong tool to recruit more and to spread their ruthless ideology around the local vulnerable Muslims, such as teens and criminal activists.

I personally spoke to many local Mosques Imams and asked them to condemn local extremists publicly but their response was not enough to make me satisfied. They replied that they fully condemn the terrorist activities of the local British Muslims who joined ISIS but they blamed the UK government for its involvement in the war in Iraq and Syria, which was a nonsense response to me. These so-called excuses generate more sympathy among the local Muslims to become extremists working against the country's political system.

They cannot provide a weak justification for not speaking out against the local extremists because it is their prime goal to speak out in public against the danger, which has shackled their religion in the UK completely. They need to start sending a powerful message to their bad guys that they have no room in their community and in Mosques by raising awareness and speaking publicly. Therefore, I strongly condemn the silent role of the British Muslim community because it is not a productive achievement to maintain peace within the community and within British society. The British society is very much doubtful of the sincerity of the Muslims living among them.

The British government needs to refine the prevent strategy according to the real on the ground strategy because the current policy has failed to deter terrorism and to detect the extremism within the Muslim community. It is a rapidly rising issue in the United Kingdom. Therefore, it needs to be solved with the help of the community. The law enforcement departments need to collaborate with the Muslim community in relations to defeating the Radicalisation. Unfortunately, there is a huge gap between law enforcement services and the local Muslim communities and none of them want to fill the gap, which is the most important way to maintain trust between each other.

The law enforcement agencies should make the human intelligence system stronger instead of fully relying on the electronic surveillance. They must recruit more capable people in order to bring about more reliable Intel reports, which can trace the coming danger of extremism. The British government should play a crucial role in order to transfer the prevent strategy to moderate and sincere Muslim Imams such as Usama Hassan, a Quilliam Foundation researcher and Tahir Mehmood, an expert on the de-Radicalisation program. These academic professionals and others like them are capable to carry out this role as part of a religious obligation and a democratic right to prevent Islamic extremism within the Muslim community.

The British government must introduce the new Counter Radicalisation Department (CRD) and that the department should provide a comprehensive training to the local Imams of the mosques, educational institutions, local community centres, etc. The CRD department must recruit moderate Muslim Imams who can provide an effective training course to the young Muslims in order to raise an awareness, deter the danger and inform about consequences if and when someone gets involved in extremism. We are living in a very dangerous situation, where we cannot trust anyone. We do not know who become a violent extremist and they start attacking our civilized values.

We need to tackle this issue very carefully and precisely. Most of the Muslim people do not know anything about Radicalisation and extremism. They are fully unaware of the rising threat of terrorism in the country. We need to teach our community that our values, dignity, identity and religious harmony is alive and stronger if we are committed to the British democratic values and we still need to integrate into British society. If we all unite, we can defeat the menace of terrorism easily but if we are divided, that will be the success of extremism and their dirty political Islamist ideology.

The Muslims Silence, an Evolution or a Solution of Extremism

On 22 May 2017, there was a devastating terrorist event after a musical concert at Manchester Arena. It was a suicide bombing that killed 22 people, mostly children, and injured more than sixty innocent people, including an eight years old child. This horrific incident was carried out by a British born Muslim extremist Salman Abedi, who was born and raised in a western world, who did not have any experience of the hardcore life of the third world countries, and who enjoyed his life full of freedom and human rights given by the British government.

This was not a new incident in Britain's tolerant society, but this type of the terrible incident happened in 2005 and it recalled the painful memories of the victims of other terrorist attacks in the UK. I burst into tears when I saw very young children with their bodies torn apart in the blast and thought how horrible Islamic terrorism is, separating the victims from their loved ones in such an atrocious way. I saw the frustration and grief in the victims' parents' eyes; they were asking questions, "What was the crime of our innocent children? Why would they have been butchered in such a merciless way?" I, being a Muslim, cannot answer their questions because I, along with other Muslims, feel that I am responsible for losing their loved ones. The very thing that puts me in an uncomfortable condition is when I see my fellow Muslims being apologetic and defensive on social media by calling this type of incident nothing to do with Islam. They are used to saying or writing a few unattractive sentences which definitely puts the parents of the victims of terrorism in a difficult situation where they cannot see Islam as a peaceful religion as they just lost their children.

"Islam is a religion of peace, Islam has nothing to do with terrorism, Islam teaches tolerance, Islam promotes love and harmony, terrorism has no religion, blah blah blah……." I am fed up with listening to these defensive comments from my own religious community because I do not see any reality in their comments. They have done nothing to prove that they are right with what they claim for.

Terrorism has a Religion, Terrorism has a Religion

Why do not Muslims understand that parents lost their children to this scum who were taking the name of Allah when blowing them up? They were chanting the *Shahadah* (creed), "There is no God but Allah and Muhammad is the messenger of Allah" while they were slaughtering innocent humans. These terrorists were worshiping the same Allah, whom we worship. They were praying and keeping fasts as all Muslims do. They were attending the mosques as we all Muslims attend on Friday and they were calling *Allah Akbar* (Allah is great) when they were killing and beheading followers of other religions, yet we claim Terrorism has no Religion!!!! Why do not we accept that Terrorists have a religion which is called ISLAM?

Most Muslims are not terrorists, but most of the terrorists involved in a religious affiliated terrorism are Muslims. Most of the Muslim population of the UK, are peaceful, democratic, pro-government individuals and against terrorism but their silence fuels the extremist ideology. I have spoken and discussed with hundreds of Muslims and everyone has some sort of justification and none of which I consider as a justification. They say "They condemn terrorism, but... they support innocent victims, but..., they are against the extremists, but...". Their BUT created extremism, their silence is not a solution but an evolution of extremism.

The Ideological Roots of Terrorism

The Manchester attacker Salman Abedi was a Muslim, The Parliament attacker Khaled Masood was a Muslim, a lone attacker who attempted to behead passenger at Leytonstone Station, Muhiddin Mire, was a Muslim, Lee Rigby murderers Michael Adebolajo and Michael Adebowale were Muslims, two men who attacked a Glasgow terminal with their Jeep burning in a fire, were also Muslims and London Underground suicide bombers Hasib Hussain, Mohammad Sidique Khan, Germaine Lindsay, Shehzad Tanweer were all Muslims. Hundreds of others who have been arrested, convicted and charged under the Terrorism Act were/are Muslims. Yet, we claim that terrorists are not Muslims and they have nothing to do with Islam is nothing but a baseless justification of their guilt. There are three fundamental beliefs within Muslims that generate extremist thoughts in their minds.

> ➢ The need to be the dominating form of Islam

> ➤ That any religions but Islam are Fake religions

> ➤ Being taught and calling other Infidels

There is a common ideological problem we Muslims have that Islam will dominate in the world. This phenomenon creates more extremism within Muslims, this is a political Islamic ideology that every nation, community and country will be defeated and dominated by Islam. This ideology leads young Muslims to become extremists and offensive towards other nations.

The real message of Islam is to live among other nations in peace, love and harmony, not with the ideology of defeating and dominating over them. The concept that all other religions are fake, changed, fabricated and Satanic except Islam, is an attitude which creates hate, extremism and a superiority complex within Muslim communities leading them to believe that they are higher than followers of other religions and that Muslims will go to paradise and the followers of rest of religion will burn into hell. This is not only an Islamic claim, but it is a political Islamic barbaric ideology which needs to be stopped immediately.

The world faces this extreme ideology that "all people, who do not believe the Prophet Muhammad (PBUH) as a messenger, are infidels and their place is in the hell fire except Muslims." This is a promotion of hate and racism towards other religions and races. Yet, we claim we are the most tolerant communities in the world!!! We not only believe in this above mentioned offensive and hatred based religious ideology, but we induce this ideology into our new generation's minds. This type of ideology fuels extremism, which leads someone to commit terrorism against the people who they consider followers of fake religions, infidels and inferiors because they think that one-day Islam will dominate in the world and Muslims will rule over them.

Solutions within the Muslim Community

This is political Islam, which drags this world into the fire with its extremist ideology and it needs to be destroyed by our own Muslim communities who need to take the prime responsibility of other Muslims' actions of terrorism. The Muslim community should stop being apologetic and defensive, but should speak up and work hard to identify this terrorist scum who are being nurtured among them.

Muslims have to take some responsibility what is happening around the world in the name of their religion. If they do not accept that responsibility, how can they change the extreme cultures of their religion! It is time to hold those who are responsible to account in order to prevent future threats to Britain and to other countries and within the Muslim community.

We Muslims, who claim ourselves as a peaceful nation in the UK, should monitor our mosques, madrasahs, homes, educational institutions, our children's behaviour, changing attitudes, their friends and any suspicious activities otherwise, we will be sitting in front of our computers, stand before other communities in a defensive situation and with apologetic behaviour by condemning terrorism We must stop saying, "Terrorism has no religion and Islam has nothing to with terrorism", instead accepting the guilt created by our own Muslim youngsters in the name of Islam who we claim to peaceful yet which still needs to be proved. My last advice to my Muslim community was that we must together cooperate with police and security services in combating terrorism. They cannot defeat this monstrous ideology without our help. They cannot enter in our religious places without any legal reason but we make them strong in protecting our children by providing intelligence of any suspicious activity within our community. We need to maintain our strong trust on our government security departments who work day and night and risk their lives to protect us and the country.

Political Islamic Terrorism, a Real Threat to the West

The terrorist attacks in the year of 2017 in London shook the entire country of England and the world because it was the third terrorist incident within three months and one which was successfully carried out by Islamists just as the holy month of Ramadan was starting. The whole Muslim community in the UK was in shock because they were not expecting these ruthless attacks to be carried out in the Muslim month-long celebration of Ramadan but the counter terrorism pundits and security service experts were expecting these incidents. The security experts in the UK believed the country may face more these types of barbaric Islamic terrorist-related attacks and it needs to be ready to counter them effectively. Muslims have to understand what real terrorism is, where it is coming from to hit the entire peaceful community in the UK, Muslims and non-Muslims alike, and where it could happen again. Muslims are living in such a very critical and hostile situation. It is one where Muslims don't see a person who one day can be your friendly neighbour and then seemingly, suddenly become a potential killer of our innocent children and someone who wants to destroy our peaceful democratic values.

That these terrorists are Muslims is not in doubt and behead our people in the name of Allah. In one of the terrorist attacks in London, one of the terrorists shouted "THIS IS FOR ALLAH" before he slit the throat of innocent people in the name of Allah. The words "ALLAHU AKBAR" have now become a symbol of terrorism and we need to accept it openly. Muslims use these words in our prayers all the time, but now Political Islamists use these sacred words to take others' lives mercilessly. This was really a big worry for the whole Muslim community across the world. There are two distinct messages of Islam being claimed by two different ideological Muslims in the world through their actions.

> ➤ Islam is one of the great religions of the world, a peaceful religion, a religion of tolerance, a religion of human rights and a foundation of world civilisations.

> ➤ Islam is a brutal, backward, barbaric religion, abusing women, violent, terrorism promoted religion, and intellectually narrow ideology that is out to annihilate civilisation.

In my opinion, both definitions of the religion of Islam are correctly being practiced worldwide. Both definitions came from the core texts of the Islamic books, one called Islamic doctrine and another called political Islamic ideology. According to Muqtedar Khan, Associate Professor in the Department of Political Science and International Relations at the University of Delaware:

> "Many Muslim intellectuals and scholars since the beginning of the colonial era and the beginning of the enduring domination of the West over Muslim countries, have been lamenting the loss of the Muslim Empire, Muslim power and Muslim glory. The key moment when the decline of Muslim power was crystallised in the Muslim psyche was when the Ottoman Empire disappeared and the Islamic caliphate as an institution was abolished in 1924. Many Islamic movements have since emerged with the explicit goal to revive the Muslim Ummah, reform Muslim societies and restore them to their past glory."

After the demolition of the Islamic Caliphate, Political Islam took over the charge to restore their lost glory by spreading Jihad in the world, by terrorising democratic societies and killing innocent people, Muslims and non-Muslims alike, in the name of Allah. They blame their lost glory to the Western powers (colonial powers) but they forget that their own religion was spreading in the world by colonising others parts of the world through Jihad. The Roman Empire, The Persian Empire, The Arab Peninsula,

The African continent and many more are examples of the Islamic colonial system.

This is the political ideology of Islam that they wish to establish their caliphate, under the heat of terrorism across the world. Now they have brought the fire of Political Islam to the streets of western democratic countries through their domestic sleeper cells. I ask a question here, who is responsible of the battle of *al-Andalusia* (Spain) when, after conquering of Spain by the Muslim Berber commander Tariq bin Ziyad, 30,000 Spaniards (including women and children) were enslaved and sent to Syria? We must read our barbaric history and not blame other nations or religions of our own crimes.

We must accept that we have manipulated the Islamic texts (Qur'an) in order to fulfil our Political Islamic desires when we dream to conquer the world under our feet through Jihad (the killing of innocents in the name of Islam). How do we define the truth that The Qur'an has 13 verses that say that a Muslim is not to be a friend of Kafirs (Infidels)? I know better that the real meaning and implementation of these verses are only in the times of war, but many Muslims in the world, whether their ideology is Political Islam or Islamic, now believe that a Muslim must not be befriended by Kafirs (Non-Muslims) under any circumstances. This is a major problem in the uneducated and illiterate of the Muslim community. It is also so in the West when they know Islam through the ideology of Political Islam and condemn that Muslims are not denouncing terrorism. But the reality is the opposite- it is Political Islam, which promotes terrorism, particularly in the streets of western countries.

According to the recent report by the UK Security services, there are around 23,000 Muslim extremists living in the UK among us and there are reports that around 450 British born Islamists came back from the war-torn zone of Syria safely and are in UK walking in the streets along with those who they consider their prime targets. This is a very critical situation for the entire population of the UK, as we never know with certainty who can be our potential killer. It's a time for Muslims living in the UK to decide that either they are in the country they born and brought up or with those who are destroying our freedom of religion, our human rights and our Islamic identity in the UK.

It's a time for Muslims not to sit in the mosques and wait for a miracle but a time to get out of your mosques, houses and make the democratic values of the UK stronger.

The British government should take some hard steps to protect the nation because according to Prime Minister Theresa May "Enough is Enough". My few suggestions to the British government:

> To increase Humint (Human Intelligence) in the security services and in the law enforcement departments because human intel is at least as, if not more effective than tech intel

> To reform prisons by separating potential terrorists into different centres

> To revoke British nationalities from the convicted naturalised terrorists

> Stop paying social benefits to extremists, Jihadists, and their families

> Close (or monitor more closely) borders

> Put suspected Islamist organisations under strict watch list

> Reform the Prevent strategy

> Introduce new counter domestic extremism policy for the prison services

The Muslim community in the UK should understand that the greatest danger in the shape of Islamic extremism has reached on their doors. These Islamists want to create a civil war between two cultures, two nations, two religions and two communities in the UK and Muslim should not let them win by not speaking out. According to my friend Matthew Cohn, a University of Frankfort professor:

> "A million Moslems should stand up in the UK and say, we have failed. We have failed our youth. We have failed to love Britain. In fact, I fear, that if the Moslem community does not rise up to root out this evil hiding in their Madrassa and holy places, Evil will smile as civil unrest and even war breaks out."

Bibliography

Abbas Au Yahya, 2011, The Religious Insurgency of the Khawarij.

Abimbola Adesoji, 2010, The Boko Haram Uprising and Islamic Revivalism in Nigeria.

Abimbola Adesojim, 2010, The Boko Haram Uprising and Islamic Revivalism in Nigeria.

Adrian Monck, 2008, Can you trust the Media.

Ahmed Rashid, 2010, Taliban.

Alison Pargeter, 2008, The New Frontiers of Jihad Radical Islam in Europe.

Ami Pedahzur, 2004, Suicide Terrorism.

Andrew Berwick, 2011, A European Declaration of Independence.

Angel Rabasa and Jeremy Ghez, 2010, Deradicalizing Islamist Extremists.

Ariel Meriar, 2004, Suicide Terrorism" in Assessment, Treatment, and Prevention of Suicidal Behavior.

Arif Jamal, 2014, Call for Transnational Jihad: Lashkar-e-Taiba.

Boaz Ganor, 2008, The Counter Terrorism Puzzle: A Guide for Decision Makers.

Brooke Barnett, 2008, Terrorism and the Press: An Uneasy Relationship.

C.M. Naim, 2008, The Mothers of Lashkar.

Charles Kegley, 1990, International Terrorism: Characteristics, Causes, Controls.

Clark McCauley, Bryn Mawr College, 2008, Pathways towards Radicalization.

Council of the EU, 2010, Instrument for compiling data and information on violent radicalisation processes.

David Satter, 2009, Yesterday Communism, Today Radical Islam.

Dr Bill Braniff, 2015, Introduction of terrorist Ideology.

Dr Boaz Ganor, 2014, The Phenomenon of Suicide Terrorism.

Ekaterina Stepanova, 2008, Terrorism in Asymmetrical Conflict: Ideological and Structural Aspects.

Errin Haines Whack, 2007, Are white shooters called "lone wolves" by default.

Ganor, Boaz, 2007, The Rationality of the Islamic Radical Suicide Attack Phenomenon.

Gary LaFree and Laura Dugan, 2009, Dynamics of Terror and Counterterrorism.

Hanif Jamez, Oliver, 2004, The Wahhabi Myth: Dispelling Prevalent Fallacies and the Fictitious Link with Bin Laden.

ICSR, 2010, Prisons and terrorism, radicalisation and De-radicalisation in 15 countries.

Intelligence and Terrorism Information Center, 2006, Suicide bombing terrorism during the current Israel Palestinians confrontation.

Jacob Zenn, 2014, Boko Haram and the Kidnapping of the Chibok Schoolgirls.

Jerrold M. Post, 1990, Terrorist psycho-logic: Terrorist behaviour as a product of psychological forces.

Jocelyn Bélanger, 2014, The Psychology of Radicalization and Deradicalization: How Significance Quest Impacts Violent Extremism.

Lee Hamilton, 2007, A Military Guide to Terrorism in the Twenty-First Century.

Magnus Ranstorp, 2009, Understanding Violent Radicalisation: Terrorist and Jihadist Movements in Europe.

Martha Crenshaw, 2000, Suicide Terrorism in Comparative Perspective, in Countering Suicide Terrorism.

Matthew Francis, 2012, What causes Radicalisation? Main lines of consensus in recent research.

Michael A. Bozarth, 2005, Terrorist Weapons and Tactics.

Musa Khan Jalalzai, 2011, The Export of Suicide Bombers.

N. D. Danjibo, 2006, Islamic Fundamentalism and Sectarian Violence: The Maitatsine and Boko Haram Crisis in Northern Nigeria.

Noor Dahri, 2014, The Evolution of Jihadism.

Richard Latter and Yonah Alexander, 1990, Terrorism and the Media: Dilemmas for Government, Journalists & the Public.

Rob Wengrzyn, 2012, Legitimate and Illegitimate Political Behavior in Organizations.

Robert A. Pape, 2003, The Strategic Logic of Suicide Terrorism.

Robert Pape, 2005, Dying to Win - The Strategic Logic of Suicide terrorism.

Roger Eatwell, 2010, The New Extremism in 21st Century Britain.

Ryan Mauro, 2014, Understanding Islamist Extremism.

Ryan McMaken, 2016, Radical Ideologies Are Only One Part of the Terrorism Equation.

Samuel P. Huntington, 1993, The Clash of Civilizations.

Sohrab Ahmari, 2015, The Ideological Islamist Threat: The radicals are waging a war of ideas the West refuses to fight.

Stanford University, 2016, The Taliban.

The Salafi Publications, 2010, The rise of Jihadist Extremism in the West.

Tinka Veldhuis and Jorgen Staun, 2009, Islamist Radicalisation: A Root Cause Model.

Tom McKearney, 2011, The provisional IRA: from Insurrection to Parliament.

Walid Phares, 2005, Future Jihad: Terrorist Strategies Against America.

Zaki Chehab, 2007, Inside Hamas.

Index

About the Author

Mr. Noor Dahri is the Founder and Executive Director of Islamic Theology of Counter Terrorism- ITCT, a UK based Counter Terrorism Think Tank. Noor was born and raised in Pakistan. He was an active member of Lahskar -e-Taibah (LeT), a Jihadist organisation in Pakistan. Noor Dahri has also worked with the London Police department for the last seven years. He has studied Forensics and Criminal Psychology from Oxford – UK, Counter Terrorism from the University of Maryland – U.S.A and also studied Counter Terrorism from International Institute for Counter Terrorism ICT- Israel. He is an independent researcher in Counter Islamic Terrorism and Islamic Extremism.

Mr. Dahri has written many research articles on the hot issues such as Counter Terrorism, Violent Extremism, De-Radicalisation and Israel-Palestine issues which have been published in various newspapers. Noor has attended many events, conferences on the threat of Counter Terrorism and also visited many institutes and libraries. Noor is a Middle East Analyst at The Great Middle East and a regular contributor at the Times of Israel (Israel) and The Daily Times (Pak). He has appeared on numerous TV and Radio shows for his interviews.

Noor is a first Pakistani, who has been officially invited to deliver his speeches at the International Institute for Counter Terrorism -ICT in Israel on the topic of "From Daw'ah To Jihad: Breaking the Radicalization and Violent Cycle". Mr. Noor is the fellow member of the Intelligence Community USA and a member of the security think tank Henry Jackson society UK. He regularly attends discussion-based events in the House of Commons and the House of Lords (UK Parliaments). He has visited many countries for his research work.

Noor Dahri received a "Life Achievement Award Certificate" by Lord Frank Judd at The House of Lords- UK in 2017.